THE DYMOCK SCHOOL OF SCULPTURE

THE DYMOCK SCHOOL OF SCULPTURE

Eric Gethyn-Jones

Phillimore

1979

Published by
PHILLIMORE & CO. LTD.
London and Chichester

Head Office: Shopwyke Hall,
Chichester, Sussex, England

*Thanks are due to the generous help of
the Marc Fitch Fund,
Bristol University and
The Bristol and Gloucestershire Archaeological Society
in enabling this volume to be published*

Printed in England by
UNWIN BROTHERS LIMITED
at the Gresham Press, Old Woking, Surrey

and bound by
THE NEWDIGATE PRESS, LTD.
at Book House, Dorking, Surrey

Contents

Cathedral; Monmouth, St. Mary's; Beckford; Stoke Orchard; Upleadon; Moccas Church (82).

List of Illustrations
following the text

Foreword

My first acquaintance with the West of England goes back to the summer of 1946, when, working on my doctoral thesis on English Romanesque Sculpture, I visited all the relevent churches of the region. It was then that I first realized that there exists a homogenous group of sculpture predating the well-known Herefordshire School and I gave a brief and rather superficial account of it in my thesis. It was, therefore, with great pleasure that I learned, some years later, that there was somebody who shared my interest in this material, somebody local, who, in addition to having an unique knowledge of the churches of the West of England, had unbounded energy and enthusiasm, and was thus ideally suited to carry out the required research of which the present book is the final outcome. The Rev. Eric Gethyn-Jones, he was not yet a Canon, has always been first and foremost a priest, whose pastoral duties had the highest priority. But he had also a passionate interest in buildings and their history, and wanted to understand the function and meaning of every architectural feature. He would climb up ladders, ledges and roofs, he has no fear of heights, to examine every stone which looked out of the ordinary. He would call in experts and put searching questions to them. He would make journeys to London to consult libraries and collections of photographs. His family holidays became study-tours of buildings in this country and abroad. Without realizing it, he became a scholar in the best tradition of the British clergy.

His M.A. thesis at Bristol University was a useful stage in his development, imposing a more rigorous historical discipline and method on his work. The present book is an abridged version of that thesis, with some changes and additions based on the author's more recent research.

It gives me a great pleasure to have been asked to write this foreword. My acquaintance with Eric Gethyn-Jones developed over the years into friendship, based on our mutual love of medieval buildings and their decoration. Our views are far from identical and there are opinions in this book to which I do not fully subscribe. But I respect the author's profound knowledge of local monuments and acknowledge that at least in one case, his dissatisfaction with the accepted opinions seems fully justified. Sir Alfred Clapham, that great architectural historian, believed that the chevron ornament, one of the most popular enrichments of the

Romanesque period, was introduced into England about 1110 and pre-dates any examples in Normandy. Canon Gethyn-Jones courageously questions this, expressing the belief that the chevron must have been known in England before 1110. I think he is right, for there is evidence that this form of decoration was known and already popular in Normandy by 1090 and, therefore, there is no reason to suppose that it was not sporadically used in England in the late 11th century.

The present book will be welcomed by students of Romanesque sculpture for focussing attention on little-known monuments of considerable interest.

George Zarnecki

Introduction

The present study is largely based on an M.A. thesis submitted to the University of Bristol some years ago. Since then it has been abbreviated and revised and much new material added. The work is primarily concerned with a group of monuments to which I have given the title The Dymock School, placing it chronologically in relation both to early post-Conquest work and to that of the Herefordshire School which succeeded it, and which continued to employ in more sophisticated forms some of the motives favoured by the Dymock School.

In the text which follows, the chronology suggested by such authorities as Sir Alfred Clapham for the principal early Anglo-Norman monuments in Herefordshire and Gloucestershire west of the Severn has, in general, been accepted. In certain instances, however, fresh evidence has demonstrated beyond reasonable doubt that new dates for particular churches or features are justified.

Hereford Cathedral is a case in point. There had been, until recently, a measure of agreement that the present building was begun $c.1107$-15. I have for many years supported those others who believed that its foundations must be attributed to Robert of Lorraine (Bishop of Hereford, 1079-95).[1] Fresh support for this viewpoint is now available.

It is possible that the evidence, both verbal and visual, contained in this narrative may suggest the need for a more general re-appraisal of the development of the art and architecture which in this area obviously preceded that of the Herefordshire School. Perhaps in time even the date for the introduction of the chevron motif into this country will need to be reconsidered.[2]

1. (a) pp.73-74.   (b) W.N.F.C. Trans., 1963, pp.316-319.
2. Sir A. Clapham, *English Romanesque Architecture after the Conquest,* Oxford, (1934), p.128.

Acknowledgments

This study owes much to the help and encouragement of a number of scholars to whom I am greatly indebted.

Special thanks are extended to the late Dame Joan Evans, to whom this work is dedicated, for shrewd advice and able guidance, to the late Professor David Talbot Rice and Dr. Michael Smith. My deepest gratitude, however, must go to Professor George Zarnecki who placed his profound knowledge of the medieval period at my disposal, and gave me the incalculable benefit of his penetrating but always friendly and constructive criticism, offered often times in a most diffident manner - an attribute perhaps of the truly great. I, naturally, am responsible for the views expressed and the errors which remain.

I am also most grateful to the undermentioned for permission to include the following illustrations and drawings.

Professor G. Zarnecki (Pl. 15 A-D).
Mrs. Myra Wilkins, the drawings of the three small confronted motifs.
Mr. David Gethyn-Jones, the cover design.

Abbreviations

Ant. J.	The Society of Antiquaries Journal
Arch.	Archaeologia
Arch. J.	The Archaeological Journal
B. & G. Arch. Soc.	The Bristol and Gloucestershire Archaeological Society
C.N.F.C.	The Cotteswold Naturalists' Field Club Proceedings
J. B. Arch. Assn.	The Journal of the British Archaeological Association
R.C.H.M.	Royal Commission on Historical Monuments (England)
V.C.H.	Victoria County Histories
W.N.F.C.	Woolhope Naturalists' Field Club

Chapter 1

The Background

The progress of christianisation of the West, the expansion of local ecclesiastical organisation and the early history of the diocese and cathedral of Hereford are uncertain. It was not, indeed, until the 8th century that the bishopric and diocese of Hereford can claim a firmly established and continuous history.

The boundaries of that medieval diocese were not clearly defined even in the 11th century, and certain parishes and districts within it were the subject of periodical litigation between the bishops of Hereford and those of Llandaff and St. David's even as late as the first half of the 12th century. It is within the southern half of that medieval diocese, today represented by the archdeaconry of Hereford and the rural deaneries of North and South Forest in the diocese of Gloucester,[1] that the majority of the monuments which form the main subject of this enquiry may be seen.

There were nine bishops of Hereford during the Anglo-Norman period, but of these three only, namely Robert of Lorraine (1079-1095), Reinhelm (1107-1115) and Robert of Bethune (1131-1148), are of importance when considering the building of the Romanesque cathedral. It was during those 70 years (1079-1148), and principally within the southern half of the diocese that three groups of sculpture, representing a chronological and artistic sequence, may be identified.

The earliest, represented by enrichments found in the churches of Bredwardine, Letton and Willersley, has no obvious affinity with either of the others. It must be examined, nevertheless, because it supplies evidence relative both to the dating of, and also to the possible sources of inspirations behind, the second group to which, as has been said, the title The Dymock School of Sculpture has now been given. The Herefordshire School of Sculpture is the third group.[2] The principal examples and the characteristics of this school are so well known that a detailed description is unnecessary. Kilpeck, that gem of 12th-century architecture, so complete and so perfect, and Shobdon, 'one of the richest and most elaborate . . . examples'[3] (but, today, a melancholy memorial to 18th-century ostentatious pride and lack of appreciation) are familiar to all students of the Norman period. Kilpeck, Shobdon and Leominster have each been suggested as the immediate source and centre of this group of sculpture, while its more remote inspiration has been attributed both to Reading and to Santiago de Compostela. Surviving examples of the work of this school are not confined to Herefordshire, but are found also in the neighbouring counties of Shropshire, Worcester and Gloucester. It is of significance, probably, that several of these churches containing monuments characteristic of this school which are outside Herefordshire once formed part of the extensive medieval diocese of Hereford, e.g., Ruardean (Glos.). This point needs to be borne in mind when considering the monuments of the other groups.

NOTES
1. These deaneries, formerly the Forest deanery of Hereford, were detached from the latter diocese on the creation of that of Gloucester in 1541. The archdeacon of Hereford, however, retained certain rights of visitation up until 1836.
2. G. Zarnecki, 'Regional Schools of English Sculpture in the Twelfth Century'. Ph.D. Thesis, London University, 1951. The first half deals with 'The Southern School' and the second with 'The Hereforshire School'. (Hereafter cited as Zarnecki (a).)
3. Sir A. Clapham, *English Romanesque Architecture after the Conquest,* (Oxford, 1934), p.126. (Hereafter cited as Clapham (b.).)

Chapter 2

Eleventh-Century Evidence

(A) DATED BUILDINGS

There are in Herefordshire and in the Forest of Dean, or in close proximity, a few buildings of an established late 11th-century date. These enable a close study of the local early post-Conquest constructional methods and sculptural enrichments to be undertaken. The three most important, although outside the specified boundaries, are sufficiently near to make it desirable that any evidence which can be derived from them should be considered. These may be briefly described in turn.

(a) Odda's Chapel, Deerhurst

Odda's Chapel, like St. Laurence Church, Bradford-on-Avon, has been recovered but recently from secular use. It is firmly dated by means of an inscribed tablet found in 1671.[1] This records that the chapel was built in 1056. The architecture of the building is not inconsistent with the tablet date. Odda's Chapel, consequently, can be taken to represent in the area under review Saxon work of the immediate pre-Conquest period, and constitutes a useful gauge at the commencement of the second half of the 11th century.

(b) Chepstow Castle

Chepstow Castle was built by William Fitz-Osbern,[2] and is firmly dated between 1067 and 1072.[3] The Great Keep, which when first constructed had only two storeys, and part of the curtain walls of the upper and middle bailies, are the most important surviving sections of the first building. The principal features which are of relevance to this analysis are to be found in or upon the walls of the Keep. They are:(a) the shallow but broad pilasters (Plate 62A), (b) the tympanum above the east doorway of the ground floor (Plate 5A) and (c) the blind arcading in the south and west walls (internal) of the second floor (Plate 5B).[4] In addition to these features there is, built into the external face of

3

of the West wall, a series of about 10 stones set on end and at an angle from the perpendicular that is suggestive of herringbone work.

(1) Doorway: The doorway has but a single order with plain jambs. The round-headed arch is of two orders, square in section, the voussoirs of which are enriched with a sunken star motif. The tympanum, made up of stones set diagonally, and its base, have the same ornamentation (Plate 5A).[5] This composite type of tympanum is found in several churches of the medieval diocese of Hereford, e.g., Churcham, Edvin Loach, Hampton Bishop, Hatfield and Letton.[6] None of these examples, however, is enriched with carving, except at Churcham where the few original infilling stones have a pattern of incised lines which have been copied upon the new material. The sunken star motif, also, is to be seen in a number of local churches, e.g., Hampton Bishop (lintel), Kempley (chancel arch) and Pauntley (chancel arch).

(a) Arcading: The arcades are blind and deep. The shafts and arches are square in section and, like the imposts, plain. The only enrichment is found at the head of the second arcade from the South in the West wall, where plaster decorated with the diagonal pattern has survived (Plate 5B). Similar decoration, but in stone, is present in the heads of the blind arcading on the outside of the south wall of the chancel at Dymock (Plate 50B).

(c) Gloucester Cathedral

The foundation stone of the Norman building was laid on 29th June 1089 and the consecration (probably of the crypt, choir and transepts only) took place on 15th July 1100.[7] In the crypt the plain cushion capital is not exclusively used. Voluted and scalloped examples occur, and upon certain voluted capitals are crude carvings. Two of these are of foliage design (Plate 6A and B), while a human head enriches the third. This last, a moustached face (Plate 6C), is not unlike the head of King Harold embroidered upon the Bayeux Tapestry in the scene in which Harold is depicted as entering the church at Bosham. There is chevron work on certain of the ribs of the crypt ambulatory. It has been suggested that settlement occurred soon after the crypt and the choir were built, and that when the vaulting was strengthened this decoration was added.[8] The figure and foliage carvings upon the crypt capitals are important, representing some of the few surviving examples of such work in the West of England which can be firmly dated late in the 11th century.[9]

The windows of the apsidal chapels in the crypt are of mid-wall design, and are similar in their outside splay to those of the 11th-century Bishop's Chapel at Hereford (Plate 45A).

(B) MATERIALS, TECHNIQUES AND DECORATIONS

In addition to the three principal monuments attention must also be given to the rôle played by local material, for the same material and techniques were not necessarily always popular; indeed quite important changes in both are to be observed. With regard to material, tufa is, perhaps, the most significant. It is present in the walling of a number of Herefordshire churches.[10] Sir Alfred Clapham and Professor Baldwin Brown pointed out that both the Romans and the Normans made use of this material, while the former authority stated that in south-eastern England it could be accepted as an indication of an 11th-century date, but that in other parts it was employed well into the 12th century, and cited Moccas church (Herefordshire) as an example of the late use of this material.[11] In most Herefordshire churches where tufa is used extensively, other features are present, e.g. herringbone work and composite tympana, which suggest an 11th-century date. Moccas, I believe, is not, as Clapham states, a mid 12th-century building, but basically an 11th-century church which received enrichments in the following century as did other local churches.[12]

The dating of herringbone work has caused much controversy in the past. Dr. H. M. and Mrs. Joan Taylor have demonstrated beyond reasonable doubt that herringbone work was employed in this country both in pre-and post-Conquest building.[13] It was widely used in Normandy in the second half of the 11th century, and numerous examples have survived from St. Wandrille (Seine Maritime) to Cerisy-la-Forêt (Manche), and continued in favour there into the early years of the next century. Its employment appears to have been confined, largely, to the churches of parochial status and not to have been used by the larger monastic houses. In Herefordshire it has survived only in the post-Conquest churches and was employed extensively during the closing years of the 11th century; and in most of these buildings there are other features which are not inconsistent with an 11th-century date, e.g., plain chancel arch, composite tympanum, tufa and the sunken star motif.

Another constructional technique employed occasionally in the area under review during the late 11th century and early 12th is that of forming the lintel or tympanum support of three stones joggled together, i.e., Hatfield (Plate 9A) and Much Dewchurch (Plate 9B). A somewhat similar formation over the west door of Castle Frome Church appears to be the result of damage and not design.

One decorative feature must be mentioned: the sunken star. This motif, varying greatly in detail, is an enrichment which was widely used. Its popularity appears to have been unusually long, extending from c. 1070 (Chepstow Castle tympanum), well into the 12th century (Pauntley chancel arch).

In brief it may be said that tufa is the one material, and herringbone
work the principal constructional method, the local employment of
which suggest a late 11th-century date. The joggled lintel stones and the
sunken star motif merely indicate the possibility of the same period.

With such dated 11th-century buildings as Odda's Chapel, Chepstow
Castle (the Great Keep) and Gloucester Cathedral crypt in mind, and with
the recognition of the enumerated constructional and sculptural details,
a beginning can be made to the study of a group of stone carvings which,
it would appear, marks an important stage in the development of local
sculpture, and which, in some measure, prepared the ground for the final
phase of Romanesque enrichment in the West, represented by the
Herefordshire School.

NOTES

1. Now in the Ashmolean Museum, Oxford. See G. Butterworth, *Deerhurst, a parish in
    the vale of Gloucester,* 2nd ed. (1890).
2. (a) Domesday; (b) J. E. Perks, *Guide to Chepstow Castle,* (Ministry of Works,
    reprint 1962).
3. (a) J. E. Lloyd, *A History of Wales, from the earliest times to the Edwardian
    Conquest,* (1911), vol. 2, p.375; (b) Bath Summer School Notes, 1962.
4. High up on the s. wall of the second storey, and close to the jamb of a window, is a
    small square stone upon which are carved crude figures. These have not, to my
    knowledge, been mentioned in any book of reference.
5. The w. doorway of Caen Castle chapel had similar constructional and enrichment
    detail (Plate 5C).
6. Only at Chepstow Castle and in the churches of Dymock and Hatfield are the stones
    set diagonally. This same diagonal pattern is employed on the turret stairway at
    Milborne Port (Plate 48D) which is dated *c.*1070 by Professor Zarnecki in the Bath
    Summer School Notes of 1962. See also H. M. and J. Taylor, *Anglo-Saxon
    Architecture,* vols.1 and 2 for suggested pre-Conquest date for these three churches-
    Dymock (pp.221-2), Hatfield (p.719) and Milborne Port (pp.424-8).
7. *Hist. et cart. S. Peter, Glou.,* vol.1, pp.11-12; Cott. MS. Dom. A. viii. fol.128;
    Dugdale, vol.1, p.543.
8. G. H. Cook, *The Story of Gloucester Cathedral,* (Plymouth, 1952), p.9.
9. The Harrowing of Hell at Bristol Cathedral is perhaps the finest piece of mid-
    11th-century sculpture in the West and is dated at *c.*1050 by Professor Zarnecki in
    English Romanesque Sculpture, 1066-1140, p.29 (hereafter cited as Zarnecki (b).
10. Mainly in two districts, (a) n.e. e.g. Edvin Loach, Tedstone Delamare and Tedstone
    Wafer; (b) Valley of the Wye, 10-15 miles w. of Hereford, e.g. Bredwardine, Letton
    and Moccas.
11. Clapham (b), p.114
12. I have considered the evidence for the date of Moccas on pp.60-63, where there is
    some amplification of this statement.
13. H.M. and J. Taylor, 'Herringbone Masonry as a Criterion of Date', in *J.B.A.A.,*
    vol.27, (1964), pp.4-13.

Chapter 3

Early Anglo-Norman Churches

There are few traces of Saxon sculpture within the area under review. The church at Stanton Lacy, the fragment of a cross shaft at Acton Beauchamp and the cross shaft and tablet at Newent are the most notable survivals.

It has been suggested that the megalithic quoins at the north-west corner of the nave wall (external) at Kilpeck, and the roughly-hewn large stones forming part of the base of the north wall of the nave at Peterstow are survivals from pre-Conquest churches.[1] In both instances it would seem that the earlier buildings were of more modest proportions than the present ones. It is, however, virtually impossible to date, even with reasonable certainty, these features. Sir Alfred Clapham's late pre-Conquest dating, consequently, is probably the most acceptable attribution.

In this study the group of churches in which herringbone work is present will first be considered.

There are in Herefordshire and in the Forest deaneries of Gloucester eight churches with herringbone-patterned masonry.[2] It is possible that some churches which have now largely or completely disappeared,[3] or others that have suffered extensive alterations,[4] once had herringbone masonry.

It is unfortunate that none of these churches where herringbone masonry is present has survived in its original entirety. All have suffered — in varying degrees — alteration or damage. In those cases where contemporary arches (Tibberton), doorways (Hatfield) or windows (Bredwardine) have undergone little or no restoration or replacement the features are usually crudely simple.

It is remarkable, remembering the extensive alterations which have

7

taken place in most Anglo-Norman churches[5] and the number of ruined or totally destroyed churches in Herefordshire,[6] (the situation in Gloucestershire west of the Severn is, on percentage, nearly as bad[7]) that so many churches retain today evidence suggestive of an 11th-century foundation. It is fortunate, too, that within the above group of eight churches there are early modifications such as the lintels at Bredwardine, Letton and Mathon, which help to throw light upon the local structural and sculptural development during the 50 years following the Conquest.

Sir Alfred Clapham said that this period was 'remarkable for its almost entire lack of ornament of any description'.[8] This statement is basically true of churches west of the Severn, for there is little in that area, with the possible exception of certain loose capitals in Hereford Cathedral,[9] that compares with the early figure or foliage work in Gloucester Cathedral or Durham Castle. The *Agnus Dei,* the pillar piscina capital and the twin-headed corbel at Preston near Dymock, the *Agnus Dei* at Byton, and possibly the 'Peter' stone at Bromyard, the tablet at Churcham, the single stone in Chepstow Castle and some of the loose capitals in Hereford Cathedral are, locally, the only sculpture having human or zoomorphic subjects which may possibly be attributed to the closing years of the 11th century.

NOTES
1.   R.C.H.M. (Herefs.), vol.1, (1931), pp.xxxvii, 156 and 217.
2.   Bredwardine, Edvin Loach, Hatfield, Letton, Mathon, Munsley, Tibberton and Wigmore. It is found, too, in the Gloucestershire churches of Ashelworth, Hartpury and Staunton, which either march with or are close to the boundaries of the Forest deanery. See pp.5-6.
3.   e.g. Flaxley Church (Glos.) was 'rebuilt' about 1730 (T. Rudge, *The History of the County of Gloucester,* (1803), vol.2, p.97), and in 1856 was 'erected' *(Little Guide - Gloucestershire* (1949) (a), p.97). Traces of a previous building, some 40 yds. from the present church may still be seen.
     Little Marcle Church (Herefs.) is a 19th-century building. There are remains of an earlier church half a mile away, while tradition tells of another at a different site. Taynton's earlier church (Glos.) was destroyed in the Civil War in 1643.
4.   e.g. Blaisdon, Minsterworth, Much Marcle, Newent, etc.
5.   The reasons for these alterations were many, but perhaps one of the most destructive was the Victorians' love of pseudo-Gothic.
6.   Brockhampton, Kynaston Chapel, Little Marcle, Tedstone Wafer, etc.
7.   Flaxley, Lancaut, Newnham, Taynton, etc.
8.   Clapham (b), p.125.
9.   See pp.13-14.

Chapter 4

Sculptural Beginnings

We pass now from the decoration by means of building techniques to that of sculptural enrichments.

There are, as already stated, three groups of churches[1] in the area under review where the Romanesque carvings in each assemblage are, obviously, related and are, presumably, the product of three workshops or bands of masons.

The earliest of these groups of sculpture is that which is found in Bredwardine, Letton and Willersley, where the lintels are enriched with, mainly, geometrical designs. The figure carving, where it exists,[2] is somewhat crude.

At Bredwardine Church (St. Andrew) the nave contains all that may be of relevance to this study. The north wall, which incorporates both external and internal herringbone work and much tufa material, has two original round-headed windows and a doorway now blocked. The doorway[3] has plain jambs and, above a plain tympanum, a round-headed arch of a single order with drip mould. All are of tufa. On both sides of this doorway is herringbone work. Inserted between the jambs and the tympanum is a decorated sandstone lintel (Plate 13A) which is, it would appear, a later addition. The west wall has an original string course below the 'restored' window.

The south wall has two original windows and an original doorway.[4] The latter has two orders; both are plain. There are nook shafts with bulbous bases, and also chamfered abaci. The plain tympanum has above it an arch of two orders; both are plain. The nook shafts are continued above the abaci, giving the effect of a moulded member attached to the outer order. All these features are of tufa. Between the jambs and the

abaci are enriched sandstone lintel (Plate 13B) and capitals. These three
stones are, undoubtedly, later additions — cf the lintel of the north
doorway.

Both lintels are enriched by shallow chip carving. The designs
employed are mainly geometrical and are similar in essence, and often in
detail, to the lintels at Letton (two and a half miles) and Willersley (four
miles). On the north doorway lintel at Bredwardine, and on the one
above the south doorway at Letton, are crude attempts at figure
sculpture, representing, perhaps, the commencement of the change, in
that area, from the geometrical to the foliage and figure designs; this
began to develop early in the 12th century and achieved its maturity in the
work of the Herefordshire School during the second and third quarters
of that century.

The Bredwardine north doorway lintel, bordered above and below by
cable moulding, and with the same pattern carved on its underside, has a
design made up of two flanking pillars, two large rosettes and two figures
within arcading.[5] A similar rosette motif is found on the sandstone lintels
at Letton and Willersley. The figures — one animal, the other possibly
human — have been the subject of considerable speculation.[6] Mr. Chester
identified them with the Egyptian gods Bes and Thoth or the Indian
elephant and ape deities. Sir Alfred Clapham describes them merely as
grotesques. Mr. Marshall and Professor Zarnecki consider the human
figure (if it is one) to be a crude example of a Christ in Majesty; the former
adds that the second figure 'represents . . . a basilisk' (Plate 17A). This
may well be so, but it is interesting to observe that a somewhat similar
twin figure design may be seen in the church of St. Genest, Lavardin
(Loir-et-Cher) near Montoire, where the large voluted capitals of the
choir arcades (north and south) have carved upon the central rectangular
panels (cf those in Gloucester Cathedral crypt) the following
figures: (1) a seated figure in the act of benediction — M. Gamard suggests
that this may be intended to be St. Benedict,[7] (Plate 17C); (2) the Virgin
and Child; (3) confronted beasts which have about them more than a
suggestion of the Bredwardine east figure, (Plate 17B). The tails of the
beasts form the twin canopy or niche. This church was built in the
11th century.[8] These two figures appear to have much in common, and
may have behind them some mutual inspiration, a view which is,
however, not shared by Professor Zarnecki.

The cushion capitals of the south doorway at Bredwardine are
enriched with linear and foliage motifs. The lintel has geometrical
decoration upon its face and underside. The motifs include variants of
the sunken star and rosette.

The main body of the nave with its tufa and herringbone work must represent a late 11th-century construction, c.1090, while the lintel and capitals were added, probably, a little later.

There is carving similar to that at Bredwardine in the neighbouring churches of Letton and Willersley. The subject matter and styles are so close that there is little doubt that they are the product of the same hand or workshop.

At Letton Church (St. John the Baptist) the nave is also basically of the 11th century. It contains all the sculptural and constructional peculiarities that are of relevance to this study.

The north wall of the nave has a crude string course of tufa on the outside and herringbone work inside. The west wall has been rebuilt, re-using much of the older material. The blocked west doorway has plain jambs, a modern lintel, reset composite tympanum and an arch of a single order (Plate 10B) — the last two features are of tufa.

The south wall, too, has been partly rebuilt, while the doorway is not quite in its original state. This doorway[9] has a moulded arch of a single order with a diapered drip mould and a composite tympanum (Plate 10A). All are of tufa. The red sandstone lintel is a 12th-century addition. The jambs are partly of tufa and partly of sandstone, the latter are 12th-century renewals. The moulding of the arch has been continued across the lintel and down the jambs and was probably carved at the time of the alterations. This is indicated by the fact that whereas the moulding on the arch is carved on the normal curve, that across the lintel and down the jamb is cut in a wide chevron pattern — a design not employed in this country, as far as is known, in the 11th-century. Furthermore, mid-way across the lintel the roll moulding is carved diagonally in the form of a cushion capital [10] and bases are formed in like manner near ground level. The flat surface of the west capital has marks upon it but its weathered condition prevents identification.

The lintel is decorated with geometrical designs similar to those on the Bredwardine and Willersley lintels (Plate 13A-D). Two of the smaller circles contain crudely-carved heads with what could be termed rayed crowns. The effect is almost that of the heads of Carausius or Allectus upon the Romano-British coins; except that the Letton heads are full-faced. The east head is that of a male; that to the west could be female. The ray effect may be no more that the pattern carved on the underside of the decoration on the lintel at Bredwardine.[11] Two other circles contain small figures. Their size, the coarse nature of the stone and its weathered condition make identification difficult. The figures appear to be shelled like a tortoise or turtle, and have heads protruding from one end and what must be tails at the other (Plate 14B).[12] An early 19th-century work on the architecture of Normandy[13] has illustrations, on plate 88, of corbels in Holy Cross Church at St.Lo. On page 105 the author writes:

'The very ancient church of St. Croix [the subject of the plates] was connected with the abbey of which little now remains. There is a tradition in the town, that it was once a temple of Ceres.' On page 107, in his account of the corbels, he continues: . . . 'and one still more rude of the mystic Scarabacus'. The figure thus described (Plate 14C) is not unlike the western figure at Letton which also has six legs. It is possible that these two have behind them a common source of inspiration. The second figure at Letton, (it has four legs), appears to be a tortoise. The presence of these figures is difficult to explain, in view of the fact that there are no parallels, as far as I know, in British medieval sculptural enrichment. It might be that, in his travels, the sculptor or the design-book artist had visited the Mediterranean lands and had seen these creatures or illustrations of them. A second suggestion is that the Letton sculptor may have been influenced in his choice of subject by Roman remains, e.g. pavements, sculpture or wall plaster decoration.[14] If this was so the small heads might, after all, be imitations of the barbarous radiates, which were common in Britain during the last century and a half of Roman rule.

A third possible identification of the four figures on the Letton lintel is suggested by an illumination on 6v of the *Chronicon Zwifaltense Minus*[15] at Stuttgart. It will be seen, if the two Letton human figures, with radiations round their heads, are compared with the medallioned moon and sun symbols cupped in the hands of Annus in the manuscript, that there is a marked similarity between the pairs. The west figure at Letton, with its pronounced hairstyle, is close in form and general appearance to the figure of the moon. The east figure at Letton has much in common with the representation of the sun. Professor Zarnecki points out[16] that this manuscript (Plate 15A) makes possible the identification of the subjects of the 31 figures (including Annus) on the outer arch above the tympanum of the west doorway at St. Lazarus, Autun. It will be observed[17] that medallions 16 and 24 of the Autun arch contain the Zodiac figures of Cancer and Scorpio (Plate 15C & D.) and are reasonably like the two animal figures at Letton (Plate 14B). The Zodiac and monthly labour figures, so common on the Continent, are only occasionally used in medieval English sculpture, e.g., the fishes at Kilpeck and the ram and fishes at Ely Cathedral. It is possible that the blank roundels at Kempley (east face of the chancel arch) may originally have been painted with similar subjects.

Of these three possible sources of inspiration for the Letton figures, i.e., the 'Barbaric radiates' for the human heads, the St.Lo corbel for either or both of the animal figures, or the Zodiac and the symbols of the Heavenly bodies in the Stuttgart manuscript for all four subjects, the last, or some similar manuscript,[18] would appear to be most likely.

Willersley Church (St. Mary Magdalene) is a single chambered building of 12th-century date and is now in a ruinous condition. It contains no tufa. The south doorway has moulded jambs and a decorated sandstone lintel. The latter is enriched with shallow geometrical carving (Plates 13D and 16A and B), and, in all probability, is by the same hand which carved the Bredwardine and Letton lintels. The carving on these four lintels constitutes a stage in the sculptural development in this area, and is of some assistance in dating its architecture.

The presence of herringbone work and the large amount of tufa at Bredwardine and Letton and the composite tympanum at the latter indicate a late 11th-century date for these buildings. The absence of these three features at Willersley suggests a later foundation for that church. In view of the great similarity of the four lintels at Bredwardine, Letton and Willersley, and of the fact that the lintels in the first two churches were, in all probability, added after the main structure had been built, it is possible that the date of the lintels represents the date of the foundation of Willersley Church. It is difficult to assess this date; but, bearing in mind the developed state of the geometrical designs, the primitive attempts at figure carving at Bredwardine and Letton, and the chevron-shaped moulding (with pseudo-cushion capitals carved upon it) on the Letton lintel and extending down the jambs, a date during the second decade of the 12th century is, perhaps, the most acceptable.

One other group of sculpture will be mentioned, but only briefly, before concluding this chapter. There were until recently several small groups of loose capitals and bases lying around in the aisles, cloisters and transepts of Hereford Cathedral. These have now been brought together in the Vicars' cloister. They vary considerably in date, but many of them are, probably, no later than the first half of the 12th century. Among the latter are some capitals of coarse sandstone on which are carved figure subjects, e.g., the Harrowing of Hell,[19] angels, etc. It is believed that certain of these are choir capitals which were replaced by Lewis Cottingham in the 19th century, and are described in vol.1 of the R.C.H.M. Herefs., p.114, as 12th-century work, presumably dating from the first period of the Romanesque building, formerly believed to be c.1110-1115.[20]

This group of loose capitals,[21] which may have relationship with other examples of Romanesque sculpture within the diocese, e.g. the 'Peter' stone at Bromyard, (Plate 4A) forms part, a vital part, of the history of the cathedral, a subject too vast to be summarised here. All that needs to be done is to record their presence and pass on to the main subject of the enquiry, namely the Dymock Group of Sculpture.

NOTES

1. The Bredwardine, Dymock and Herefordshire. It is interesting to observe that the majority of the more important monuments of these groups are found on one side of an imaginary line passing n-s. through the city of Hereford. The first and third to the west, and the Dymock to the east.
2. Bredwardine and Letton.
3. R.C.H.M. (Herefs.), vol.1, p.25. See also Plate 83A.
4. *Ibid.*, Plate 83B.
5. The chamfered underside of much of the carving at the top of the lintel has shallow incised lines forming a type of chevron design.
6. G.I. Chester, 'Notice of Sculptures of Oriental Design at Bredwardine and Moccas, Herefordshire', in *Arch. J.*, vol.47, (1890), pp.140-42; Sir A. Clapham in R.C.H.M. (Herefs.), vol.1, p.26; G. Marshall, 'Remarks on a Norman Tympanum at Fownhope, and others in Herefordshire', in W.F.N.C. *Trans.* (1918), p.57, (hereafter cited as Marshall (a)); Zarnecki (a), pp.222-3.
7. R. Gamard, *Lavardin, Montoire, Saint Jacques,* Zodiaque series No.34, no date, pp.16 and 102.
8. *Ibid.* The date given for these pillars is *c.*1040 — see plan and p.10 M.P. Lavedan, *French Architecture,* (1956), translation, p.94, dates a St. Gilderic at Lavardin 'from 1042'. Is this a second church in Lavardin? If so I have to find it. Might this be an alternative dedication for St. Genest?
9. R.C.H.M. (Herefs.), vol.3, Plate 146.
10. A similar motif is carved upon the e. capital of the s. doorway at Moccas.
11. See above, note 5.
12. R.C.H.M. (Herefs.), vol.3, p.134, terms them 'toad-like forms'.
13. J. S. Cotman, *The Architectural Antiquities of Normandy,* (1822), 2vols.
14. Letton is less than 10 miles from the site of the Roman town of Magna (Kenchester), and less than 40 miles from the large Roman centres of Caerleon and Gloucester.
15. G. Zarnecki, *Gislebertus: Sculptor of Autun,* (Paris,1961), pp.24 and 29, (hereafter cited as Zarnecki (f)).
16. *Ibid.,* p.29.
17. *Ibid.,* Plate B and appendix pp.30-31.
18. e.g. St. John's College, Cambridge, Library MS. B.20 (Worcester). There is no positive evidence for a medieval scriptorium at Hereford Cathedral. A manuscript bought by, or given to, the cathedral library, and now lost, could, however, have been the inspiration behind the carving of those figures.
19. Zarnecki, (b), Plate 27.
20. Clapham (b), pp.126-7.
21. See below pp.8 and 72-73.

Chapter 5

The Dymock Group of Sculpture

(a) The Motifs

There is, some distance eastward of the Bredwardine group, a considerably larger number of churches containing obviously related works of sculpture. Individual monuments of this group have long been accepted as earlier in date than the works of the Herefordshire School.[1] The main concentration of these carvings is within a 10-mile radius of Dymock. 'Wanderers', however, are found as far north as High Ercall (north-east of Shrewsbury), but all except the latter are within the boundaries of the medieval diocese of Hereford. To this group has been given the title The Dymock School, firstly because its church is at the centre of the area and is the largest ecclesiastical building containing such carvings,[2] and secondly because fine examples of the three distinctive motifs of the group, one in its most elementary form, are found in Dymock.

There can be seen, when studying the monuments of this group, changes in the quality of workmanship and modification in the designs employed. This suggests a continuity of direction over a period of years which, in turn, may assist when the problem of dating is considered.

There are within 20 miles of St. Mary's Church, Dymock, the following examples of the principal motifs favoured by this local workshop:

(a) Five tympana and a font decorated with the same distinctive tree motif.[3]

(b) Nine churches containing capitals enriched with the large stepped volutes peculiar to this group of sculpture.[4]

(c) Three churches where small confronted volutes, closely related yet differing in detail, are present.[5]

(d) There are also several churches where a stepped pattern, divorced

15

from volutes, is found. It is carved upon some capitals, usually of the cushion variety which are plain or enriched with a simple semi-circular border (Eldersfield—Plate 38A & B), and is seen, occasionally, upon other parts of the structure or pieces of furniture, e.g., lintel (Much Dewchurch—Plate 9B), figure design (Deerhurst—Plate 37A), font (Stoke Orchard — Plate 39A) or string course (St. Mary's Church, Monmouth—Plate 34C).

There are, further afield, other examples of these motifs, e.g. tympana—High Ercall (Shropshire) and Rochford (Worcestershire but formerly Herefordshire), confronted volutes — Cusop, Leominster and Rowlstone — all Herefordshire. A catalogue of relevant monuments was included in the original thesis. See p.86.

A preliminary examination of the motifs themselves must now be undertaken.

Mr. C. E. Keyser, in his mongraph of *Norman Tympana and Lintels* (2nd Ed., 1927), expressed the belief that though some tympana undoubtedly date from Saxon times, 'most of them belong to the Norman period of architecture, say: 1080-1200'. Sir Alfred Clapham appears to agree with this statement, but Professor Zarnecki is of the opinion that note is Saxon.

It is apparent that certain areas occasionally favour a common motif and that local sub-divisions, which may represent the work of individual masons or workshops, may sometimes be detected. The distinctive tympanum motif of the Dymock group, often described as 'The Tree of Knowledge and Spiritual Life', represents such a sub-division, which might be termed a West Midland enrichment.

Mr. Keyser details 41 examples of tympana in which a tree occupies a prominent place. The Yatton (Plate 21A) and Hereford Cathedral[6] (Plate 18C) examples increase the number to 43. The county of Gloucester has seven such tympana (four east of the Severn[7] and three west), Herefordshire four, Shropshire four, Worcester two and Radnor one. Of these the three Gloucestershire examples west of the Severn (Dymock, Kempley and Newnham), the four in Shropshire (Buildwas (Plate 21C), High Ercall (Plate 19A), Morville and Tugford) and one each of the Herefordshire and Worcestershire specimens (Yatton (Plate 21A) and Rochford (Plate 20C) show a striking similarity, while the cathedral tympanum motif might well be the local prototype, and the Kilpeck tree or vine (Plate 21B) a variant carved by a sculptor of the Herefordshire School.[8] The remaining Herefordshire example is at Moccas (Plate 60A). A religious significance has often been attributed to the tree motif, e.g. a representation of the cross of man's salvation, the true vine (St. John ch.15) or a palm tree symbolic of immortality.[9]

There are within this group of churches four other tympana with carved motifs, and two which are almost plain: (1) Agnus Dei at Preston (Plate 23A) and Upleadon (Plate 24A), (2) squared stones with cross-hatched lines at Churcham (Plate 9D) and (3) overlapping scale pattern at Pauntley (Plate 28B). The pair of tympana, composed of squared stones set diagonally, at the head of the two panels of blind arcading at Dymock (Plate 50B) must also be recorded.

Symbolism was extensively employed in Christian art throughout the centuries, with the Agnus Dei second only in popularity to the Cross as an enrichment for the tympana of the Anglo-Norman churches.[10] The significance of the Agnus is not easy to determine. There are six churches in or near the area being considered where the Agnus is carved upon their tympana,[11] but of these Preston near Dymock alone is dedicated to St. John the Baptist. The Apocalyptic Lamb is probably intended where 'supporters' are present, while St. John, ch.1, vv.29-36 *(Ecce Agnus Dei)* may have inspired others. Keyser records 32 tympana with this motif.

The voluted capital is of classical origin. It was widely imitated in Western Europe during the cultural revival of the 11th and 12th centuries, when it underwent, at times, considerable modification; a process reflected in many directions, and which may have prompted Professor Morey to feel that Romanesque art 'reflects the gradual sinking of Latin culture below the Celtic and Teutonic surface'.

The typical Norman and Anglo-Norman volute is bulbous in body and is formed by a single arm or leaf curved within itself. At Dymock, however, and in most churches of this group, the volute, initially, has three arms: one fades into the abacus, a second joins its fellow from the other face of the capital and forms the stepped pattern or tongue (Plate 28A), while the third member makes about two and a half coils as the volute. It is noticeable too that the volute at Churcham, Dymock, Fownhope (north and south windows of the third stage of the central tower), Pauntley (south doorway) and Yatton is essentially a flat incised figure. The volute at Bridstow, Bulley, Kempley, Newnham and Pauntley (chancel arch) is slightly more bulbous in form. Both groups are so unlike the normal Anglo-Norman volute that an explanation is called for. Spiral motifs occur in the art of several periods and of many countries, but the flat incised sculptural examples on the capitals of the Dymock group are peculiar, today, to this area. It is possible that a local mason or masons responsible for those capitals interpreted the ordered volute motif in a form familiar to and favoured by his forefathers.

The stepped pattern found in conjunction with the Dymock type of volute,[12] and also seen in relief in other settings,[13] is, obviously, a motif surviving from pre-Conquest days.[14]

First stage   Second stage   Third stage

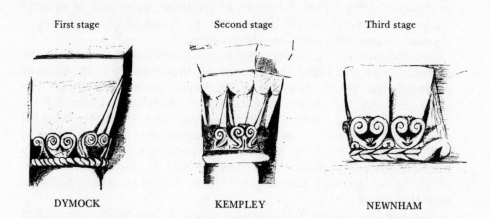

DYMOCK   KEMPLEY   NEWNHAM

The churches of Dymock, Kempley and Newnham contain examples of the tympanum motif and the large stepped volute characteristic of the Dymock sculptural group. There is in the above churches yet a third common motif, namely the small confronted volute. These volutes in Dymock Church, rising from the necking band of the plain cushion capitals on the nook shafts of the two surviving square pillers of the original central tower (Pl. 32A),[15] are crudely simple. Those at Kempley are on the scalloped capitals of the nook shafts of the south doorway in the nave (Plate 32B), but, unlike those at Dymock, they have no break between each pair. The volutes (the pairs are equidistant from each other) have no contact with the necking band, but are a little above it. The Kempley examples have two additional features, i.e.; (1) a small squat 'T' situated between each confronted pair, with the vertical member resting upon the apex of two volutes, which may be intended to be a type of step pattern; and (2) a small triangular feature formed by the backward extension of the stems of the two volutes. The volutes thus joined by the triangular feature could well be considered a stylised ramshead (Plate 32B).

The third example is on a loose capital at Newnham-on-Severn. Here, although basically the pattern is the same, there is a marked difference in the character of the additional features. The spirit of the flowing curves of the small volutes has taken possession of the 'T' and triangular motifs. Gone are the straight edges and hard lines, and in their place are gentle bends and undulations. The body of the 'T' is concave, and its horizontal member ripples like the sea. The triangular feature is treated in a similar manner. Finally the necking band is carved in a plaited pattern.

This concludes the preliminary study of the characteristic works of sculpture of the Dymock group. Each of the three motifs is distinctive and all have a very restricted area of distribution.[16]

Its Date — a preliminary survey

The *termini ante quem et post quem* for the Dymock group of sculpture are generally accepted, but widely separated. It is acknowledged that the Dymock and Kempley tympana antedate that at Kilpeck.[17] The latter church was given by Hugh, son of William the Norman, to St. Peter's Abbey, Gloucester, in 1134.[18] Consequently this must be the *terminus ante quem* for the work of the Dymock group.

The two unusual types of volutes found on the capitals of this group, although differing in form, are both suggestive of a ram's head, the larger ones particularly so. One of the loose capitals assembled in the Vicars' Cloister in Hereford Cathedral, said to have come either from the Bishop's Chapel of Robert of Lorraine (1079-95) or from the eastern portion of the cathedral (Plate 26A & B)[19] (part of which is also attributed by some authorities to Robert[20]) has a crude ram's head carved on two faces, with the horns giving a volute-like effect. There is no trace, however, of a tongue, real or simulated, such as is found for example on the Dymock south doorway capitals. In spite of this omission it seems possible that the inspiration behind those capitals came via the cathedral. This would give 1079 as the *terminus post quem*. The presence of chevron work found in conjunction with many of the tympana and capitals of the Dymock group considerably closes the gap between the *termini*. Sir Alfred Clapham firmly dates the appearance of the chevron in this country at Hereford at between 1110 and 1115.[21] Most authorities agree.[22]

A subdividing of the date-bracket for the Dymock group of sculptures seems to be possible through an apparent three-stage development in certain monuments.

There are more than a dozen churches in the group,[23] of which eight contain two or more examples of this sculpture. These are: Bridstow, Bulley, Dymock, Fownhope, Kempley, Newnham-on-Severn, Pauntley and Yatton.[24] In each of these, and also in Churcham and Preston, there are examples of the large stepped volute. They differ slightly in their form, but basically they are the same design, inspired by the same source, and came perhaps from one workshop. These differences may have significance.

There are tympana also in seven of these eight churches. Four of the tympana[25] are enriched with a similar design, i.e. the tree or foliage. The fifth, Pauntley, has a scale pattern (Plate 56A). The Bulley one is plain save for a little moulding, while that at Fownhope (Madonna and Child or Trinity),[26] now built into the west wall (internal) of the nave, is a work of the Herefordshire School.[27] It has been stated that in three of these churches[28] there are small confronted volutes, similar in basic design but showing a gradual advancement in workmanship from the plain unimaginative to a sophistication that is suggestive, almost, of the Herefordshire School. These capitals with the confronted volutes and the piscina capital from the Preston, upon which are carved crude rams' heads with stepped tongues, appear to be the key to any attempt at dating the sculpture of the Dymock group. The earliest surviving monuments of the group will be found in Dymock, Preston and Bromyard.[29]

It is proposed to consider first Preston, with particular reference to the tympanum and the pillar piscina capital, and next to examine Dymock, basically an early Anglo-Norman church.[30] St. Mary's, Kempley, will then be studied, and, finally the loose fragments of Romanesque sculpture in Newnham Church — obvious survivals of an earlier building.

It is thus hoped to establish a chronological sequence for the sculpture peculiar to the Dymock group.

NOTES

1. Zarnecki (a), pp.223-29; T.S.R. Boase, *English Art, 1100-1216,* (Oxford, 1953), p.81.
2. I have excluded Bromyard. The church there is later in date than the font which alone in that building shows affinity with the sculpture of the Dymock Group.
3. Dymock, Kempley, Newham, Rochford and Yatton. The font is at Bromyard.
4. Bridstow, Bulley, Churcham, Dymock, Fownhope, Kempley, Newnham, Pauntley and Preston, near Dymock.
5. Dymock, Kempley and Newnham.
6. See below, pp.73-74.
7. Dowdeswell, Lower Swell, Siston and Stratton.
8. Thus 11 of the 13 examples of the tympanum tree motif in this area appear to have behind them a common inspiration.
9. (a) C.E. Keyser, *Norman Tympana and Lintels in the Churches of Great Britain,* (2nd ed., 1927), pp.xxxvi-ii, (hereafter cited as Keyser (d)); (b) B. & G. Arch. Soc. *Trans.,* vol.31, p.2.
10. Keyser (d), p.lix.
11. See below p.22.
12. e.g. Bulley, Dymock, Kempley, Pauntley, etc.

13. e.g. Madonna and Child at Deerhurst, Hereford Cathedral nave capital, Eldersfield chancel and s. doorway capitals, Llanbadern Fawr lintel, etc.

14. i.e. Roman occupation, e.g. Woodchester mosaics; Saxon period, e.g. MS. illustration (Book of Kells and Lindisfarne Gospels), metal ornamentation (Sutton Hoo treasures), sculpture (Deerhurst Madonna). Professor Baldwin Brown, *Anglo-Saxon Architecture,* pp.281 and 427, writes of the 'traditional Saxon step-pattern ornament'.

15. This feature no longer exists.

16. See figures, p.18.

17. (a), Zarnecki (a), p.279, (b) Boase, *op. cit.,* p.81.

18. Dugdale, *Monasticon,* vol.1, p.548.

19. A 19th-century 'replacement' capital of similar design is to be seen on the n. side of the presbytery which suggests that the older one came from the cathedral and not the chapel.

20. See below, pp.73-74.

21. Clapham (b), p.128

22. I am not entirely happy with this assessment, and feel that when a further detailed study of the cathedral is made, an earlier date for the first appearance of the chevron may have to be accepted.

23. Bridstow, Bromyard, Bulley, Churcham, Dymock, Fownhope, High Ercall, Kempley, Newnham, Pauntley, Preston, Rochford and Yatton.

24. Kempley and Pauntley march with Dymock, Yatton with Kempley, while Bridstow and Fownhope are only a few miles from Yatton - see map.

25. Dymock, Kempley, Newnham and Yatton.

26. See below, p.46.

27. Fully described by Professor Zarnecki, (a), pp.337-42.

28. Dymock, Kempley and Newnham.

29. The font only in this church, and possibly, the small tablet above the n. doorway in Churcham Church.

30. Dr. H. M. Taylor and Dr. C. A. Raleigh Radford, while accepting the two-stage development of the sculpture in Dymock Church, disagree with the dating for the earlier parts of the building as set out in this study. Dr. Taylor described this work as basically mid-11th-century pre-Conquest *(Anglo-Saxon Architecture,* vol.1, (1965), pp.221-22). This opinion he re-affirmed in person at Dymock in 1965. In 1965 Dr. Raleigh Radford also revisited Dymock Church. Later that afternoon he made it clear that he supported Dr. Taylor's statements, and considered a late 11th-century date for such features as the blind arcading and pilasters at Dymock to be unacceptable. I feel, however, that the weight of evidence *is* in favour of the later date. Professor Zarnecki agrees. Dr. Taylor has also pointed out that there is an early example of the confronted volutes at Stoughton (Sussex) (vol.2 Plate 583). This pair is considerably larger than those at Dymock, Kempley and Newnham and moreover, is an isolated pair, while those considered in this study are pairs in *series* round parts of three sides of five capitals - a totally different matter.

Chapter 6

The Dymock Group of Sculpture

The Churches
Preston Church (St. John the Baptist)

The walls of the north-west corner of the nave of Preston Church contain all the surviving Romanesque work (excepting a loose piscina capital now in Gloucester museum). The tympanum over the north doorway has an Agnus Dei (Plate 23A) carved upon it that is much inferior to those at Aston (Hereford), (Plate 24B), Gloucester, St. Nicholas (Plate 24C) and Upleadon (Glos.) (Plate 24A). It is, indeed, as crudely carved as the only other local examples, i.e., at Byton (Hereford) (Plate 23B) and Castle Morton (Worcs.) (Plate 23C). In these last three instances the lamb is kneeling, and at Preston the folded left fore-foot supports a pole surmounted by a circular Maltese Cross.

Byton Church was rebuilt in 1859/60 incorporating some old material including the tympanum. Here the Agnus is flanked by two incised examples of the knot motif, (Plate 23B), an enrichment common in Celtic decoration, and also found locally upon a re-used stone built into the south-east buttress of the chancel of Llangarron Church (Hereford) (Plate 40C). The Byton tympanum has been described by Sir Alfred Clapham as 'probably of late 11th or early 12th century date'.[1]

The tympanum at Castle Morton is similar in general design to that at Preston. The border above the motif in both instances is marked off by incised lines into voussoir-like divisions. At Castle Morton the tympanum is set within an arch enriched with an outward-turned chevron motif — a strange combination that is probably explained by the insertion of the decorated arch at a later date, a practice which seems to be not infrequent in the area under review.[2]

The square jambs of the doorway at Preston, without capitals or pronounced imposts, are plain and match the general simplicity of the whole unit for which a late 11th-century date would seem realistic. Professor Zarnecki is prepared to accept this possibility.

22

The loose piscina capital[3] probably formed part of the furniture of this early Preston Church and is important evidence for the dating sequence within the Dymock group of sculpture and for the sources of inspiration behind it. The capital is four-sided, hollowed out and with a central drain hole. It is enriched upon its four corners with the stepped volute characteristic of the group. The necking band is plain and from it rise fleshy leaves like scales reversed with, on each side, a central spear-head motif. From the flanking leaves spring lines which curve towards the corners, where are carved rams' heads from which protrude tongues cut into a step pattern (Plate 27C). The workmanship is comparable with that at the north doorway, and is not inconsistant with a late 11th-century date.

The twin heads of the corbel at the north-west corner of the nave (Plate 27C) are similar to those carved upon a capital at Durham Castle chapel and upon the tympanum at Barton Seagrave and are, presumably, contemporary with the Preston tympanum and pillar piscina.

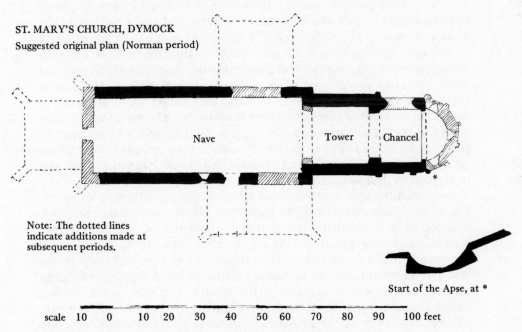

ST. MARY'S CHURCH, DYMOCK
Suggested original plan (Norman period)

Nave

Tower   Chancel

*

Note: The dotted lines indicate additions made at subsequent periods.

Start of the Apse, at *

scale 10   0   10   20   30   40   50   60   70   80   90   100 feet

Plan drawn by F. W. Waller, Esq. Reproduced by courtesy of Colonel N. H. Waller, M.C., T.D. and the Cotteswold Naturalists' Field Club

Dymock Church (St. Mary)

Dymock Church had, originally, four divisions, i.e., apse, a short chancel, a (square) central tower and a high narrow nave. The transepts, north and south, present problems. They are set irregularly, with the north member sited nearer to the west. The rounded arches, which have the appearance of being original, are of a single order (square in section) with plain squared imposts and jambs.[4] The three faces of each jamb retain evidence of dressing. The east and west walls of the transepts are not bonded into the nave wall suggesting that the present transepts are of a latter period. The features within, e.g., windows and piscina, are also of a post-Anglo-Norman date. There is no trace of sculptural work upon the arches; consequently the problem of the transepts[5] must be left and a return made to the main subject.

The apse was not of the rounded form found locally at Moccas and Peterchurch, but polygonal, and was, seemingly, enriched with blind arcading. The traces of this apse which remain are confined to the responds north and south where the blind arcading of the chancel turned to form the polygonal east end. The respond on the north side, now within the priest's vestry, added in 1870, is intact from a height of approximately eight and a half feet to about a foot and a half above the nook capitals. The chamfering and angle of the first bay of the arcading of the destroyed apse can be seen on both the fragment of the arch springing from the respond and also down the east side of the respond itself. The nook capitals are of the cushion pattern. The two surfaces of the head of the respond — the north and the chamfered — between the nook shaft capitals are decorated with shallow incised vertical lines placed close together. The corresponding respond on the south wall is complete (exterior face), and shows that the chamfering is continued through the string course to ground level, leaving no doubt that the apse was polygonal in design (Plate 50B and C). Sir Alfred Clapham was of the opinion that the apse was five-sided.[6] The Gloucester diocesan architect, Mr. F. W. Waller, held the same view.[7] Sir Alfred also said that Dymock was the only Norman parish church in England, of which he knew, possessing a polygonal apsidal east end. The apse, common in Normandy and France generally, did not supplant in this country the rectangular form favoured by native craftsmen. Sir Alfred, commenting on the distribution in England of the apsidal east end in the smaller parish churches, said that it 'was more frequent in the south-eastern part of the country'.[8] Mr. Fairweather supports this statement with the following figures:[9] Essex 15, Norfolk 10, Suffolk six, Kent seven and

Sussex five, whereas the figures for the west are small, e.g., Lancashire two, Shropshire three, Gloucestershire (excluding Saxon Deerhurst and the recently discovered Saxon example at Cirencester) two, and one each in Cornwall, Devon, Somerset and Worcester. In Herefordshire however, there are eight. In addition one of the two Gloucestershire examples, Dymock, was within the medieval Hereford diocese. This is remarkable. What reason could there have been for the polygonal form of the Dymock apse? Might it have been more than an ordinary parish church? The Flaxley Abbey Cartulary (deed No.49 c.1190) contains the phrase: 'de monasterio de Dimmoc'.[10] Domesday records that Dymock was a royal possession at that time, and, statistically, was a place of some size.[11] It is possible that the collegiate status suggested by the Flaxley Cartulary may have existed and may have been enjoyed a century earlier.

Dymock chancel has suffered much damage and alteration. On the north side (external) the broken respond within the 19th-century priest's vestry alone remains. More has survived (externally) of the south wall. A string course, at a height of six and three-quarter feet, divides the wall into two zones; the upper is decorated with blind arcading of which two bays to the east remain.[12] The arches are of a single order, square in section, and their heads are filled with square stones set diagonally. The responds of this arcading have cushion capitals at the head of the nook shafts and plain moulded bases. Inside the chancel the surviving features of the original structure are the broken rectangular responds of the arch which separated the chancel from the apse and a short length of string course (cable pattern) west of the north respond, and a shorter one with different enrichment built into the south wall above the window next to the modern screen. The responds are intact to a height of eight feet, and have small nook shafts east and west, with semi-bulbous moulded round bases. Those on the north respond are enriched with a spur motif at the corners (Plate 55C). The bases on the south have an overlapping scale pattern (Plate 55B), such as is found upon the tympanum of the South doorway at Pauntley and upon the font at Llantwit Major (Glamorgan). The diagonal pattern of the stones in the head of the bays of the blind arcading are, as has been said (see p.4), similar in design to that in the head of one of the bays in the Great Keep of Chepstow Castle (c.1071) and in several local tympana, e.g., Chepstow Castle and Hatfield Church, and in the external stairway at Milborne Port (Plate 48D), all of which are of post-Conquest 11th-century date.[13]

The third chamber of the church, the central tower (19ft x 19ft), retains many of its original features. The south wall (externally) is intact up to the string course (9ft. 6in.) with shallow pilasters (13in. by 1½in.) set at

intervals. The easternmost pilaster extends through the string course to a
height of approximately 20 feet. The string course, which here is nearly
three feet higher than that on the chancel well, is heavy and has
geometrical patterns carved on it. The flat outer face of the upper zone
has an oblong design bisected diagonally by a single line (Plate 35C). The
lower zone (two-thirds) is moulded and has upon most sections a
confronted incised chevron design (Plate 35C). Variations of this pattern
occur, especially where the string course passes over the pilasters. The
only major departure, however, is on two sections of the central tower
block. In these instances the lower zone has a plain cable pattern similar
to that upon the two sections west of the broken north respond inside
the chancel (Plate 36B).

The central tower, on the inside, retains the square responds which
supported the east wall of the tower and from which an arch, earlier than
the existing one, sprang. The west corners of these responds have large
nook shafts, the bases of which are moulded. That to the north is
enriched with the spur motif similar to those upon the nook shafts of the
broken north respond between the chancel and the apse now
destroyed.[14] The capitals of these tower shafts are of cushion design and
have cable necking bands from which rise small paired confronted
volutes (Plate 32A). The carving is competent but simple and
undeveloped in design. Small volutes, set in series, are found in the
decoration of many countries, for example, France.[15] Confronted pairs
in continuous pattern are found not only in Dymock but also in Kempley
and Newnham. These three examples show a gradual development of
design. There are also in certain Herefordshire churches carved motifs
which are, essentially, the same, but treated with greater elaboration.[16]
At the west end of the north wall of the central tower block is a small
narrow doorway. The door is set within the wall with rebate on the
church side, and drawbar and socket behind the door. The hollowed
chamfering of the north-east end of the passage through the wall (Plate
48B) leaves no doubt that it gave access to an external stair turret such as
has survived at Milborne Port in the angle between the south transept
and the nave (Plate 48D), and also at Ledbury,[17] Herefordshire. The
latter turret appears to have been rebuilt or refaced comparatively soon
after its completion. The jambs of the Dymock doorway are plain and
square. Two crude imposts have been built into the west jamb, but
neither is in contact with the tympanum above the doorway. This
tympanum (Plate 48A) is an oblong stone upon which has been carved in
relief near the base a plain band. A shallow incision separates this band
from a rounded moulding which extends the full length of the

tympanum. The two ends of the latter are linked by a broad semi-circular band in relief which is divided (as at Preston) by incised lines into eight voussoir-like segments. The whole is a tympanum of simplicity, and is some what similar to its counterpart at Ledbury (Plate 48C). In the latter church the original Anglo-Norman nave was replaced by a narrow one in the 13th century. Four of the bases of the arcade pillars of the earlier building survive (Plate 61B). It is possible that the original Anglo-Norman Ledbury Church — implied in Domesday — and the earlier portions of Dymock Church were contemporary.

The north wall of the nave at Dymock has two complete pilasters surviving and four broken ones (Plate 55A). Two of the latter formed the jambs of the original north doorway, and have the inside edges chamfered. A 19th-century window has destroyed the head of this doorway. Close to the east jamb a plain voussoir stone has been built into the wall. A short length of string course, plain with chamfered lower half (Plate 36A), has survived.

The south wall of the nave retains three intact pilasters, including the pair which has been incorporated into the jambs of the south doorway, and portions of three others. A seventh forms the south-east corner of the nave where the narrower central tower block begins. A length of string course has survived west of the south doorway and is enriched with the commoner motif. There is, in the south wall, west of the south doorway, a round-headed window. This window (Plate 35D) has an arch of two plain moulded orders and nook shafts with cushion capitals and moulded bases.

The south doorway, a fine example of Anglo-Norman workmanship (Plate 19B), may well contain the key to certain of the dating sequence problems connected with the Dymock group of sculpture. The doorway, today, has a tympanum design common to several churches within this group, and capitals with the large stepped volute motif found in even more of these buildings. [18] The doorway is sited between a pair of pilasters which are matched and which differ from all the others surviving. They measure 19in. by 2in. as compared with 13in. by 1½in., occasionally almost 13½in. by 2in.

The panel between this pair is approximately 7ft.3in., of which 3ft.10in. is taken up by the door space. This leaves a further 3ft.5in. to be considered. It will be noticed that the jambs of the outer order are a continuation of the pilasters both in regard to surface and the nature of much of the stone, i.e., old red sandstone of a mainly greyish colour. The measurement on the west side of the doorway[19] from the pilaster's edge (west) to the extremity of the capital or base is 3ft.0½in., compared with the 19in. of the pilaster above the doorway.

The doorway is of two orders. The outer has nook shafts carved from the jamb corners. These shafts lie within the surface limits of the jambs; i.e., the capitals, necking band and bases are on the same vertical plane, with no protrusion at any point. The shaft capitals have stepped volutes typical of the group, and the bases are bulbous and have primitive spurs. The inner order has shallow and slender nook shafts with cushion capitals which, again, are contained within the jamb faces. Between these shafts and the angle with the outer order is a hollow moulding. Above the capitals of the outer order is a narrow strip of stone-work which protrudes a little, giving the impression of a shallow hood mould or string course. The upper zone is flat and enriched above with a variation of the bisected rectangle motif on the main string course, and below a shallow incised zig-zag decoration. The lower zone of the stone strip is shaped in a concave chamfer. It is in reality an extension of each abacus. It is noticeable that the actual abaci and a section of the extension on either side of the doorway are made up of stone of a different shade and perhaps nature from that forming the extremities. The chamfering, too, of the inner portions is narrower, causing an uneven join at the point of union. It would seem from the general appearance that the extremities are the original sections.

The tympanum has the Tree of Life motif carved beneath a double row of pellets and a hollow mould. The arch has chevron work, and the hood mould has the same enrichment as upon the upper zone of the main string course.

The doorway area, at first sight, appears original. It will be observed upon close inspection, however, that the arch above the tympanum, indeed the whole tympanum unit, has been 'let in' at, it must be assumed, a date after that of the main building.

The west pilaster has been cut away, in a curve for more than half its width, to accommodate the hood mould and part of the arch where it completes its downward curve on the west side. It would appear that some difficulty was encountered when the tympanum unit was inserted.

Stone 1 of the pilaster is shaped and bonded into the nave wall to the west, but its edge, where it forms part of the pilaster, now breaks the downward line (point A). The joint, too, between the hood mould and the pilaster is irregular, and the lowest stone of the hood mould shows damage. It would appear that the stone marked 1 was taken out for the insertion of the tympanum unit, and that when the stone was replaced it was not found possible to return it quite to its former position — hence the protrusion westwards.[20] The roof of the later porch hides, very largely, the corresponding feature on the East side, but, as far as it is possible to judge, the same general conditions prevail.

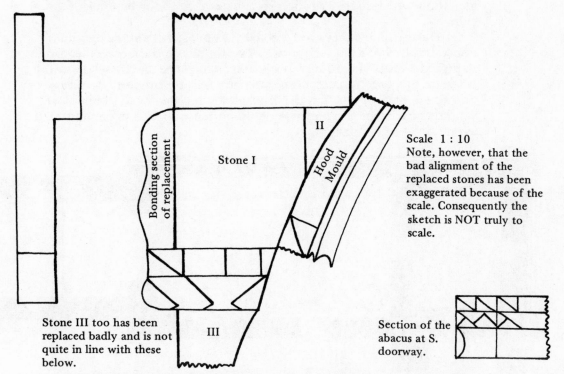

Bonding section of replacement

Stone I

II

Hood Mould

Scale 1 : 10
Note, however, that the bad alignment of the replaced stones has been exaggerated because of the scale. Consequently the sketch is NOT truly to scale.

Stone III too has been replaced badly and is not quite in line with these below.

III

Section of the abacus at S. doorway.

It should be noted, too, that the string course, which in every instance on the outside walls, south and north, overrides each pilaster, comes part-way across the west pilaster forming the west door-jamb, and is cut away in a diagonal curve to allow the insertion of the tympanum unit.

It might be suggested that the doorway did not form part of the original church. The fact that the internal and external measurements of this doorway and those of the blocked doorway of the north wall are almost identical (4ft.6in. internal and 3ft.10½in. external), and that both doorways are sited between pilasters which seem to be paired, [21] indicated that this theory is untenable.

Could it be that the original South doorway was altered at a later date to accommodate a tympanum unit, or a newer one? It is inconceivable, had the tympanum and arch formed part of the original design, and observing the finish of the pilasters, string course and blind arcading, that the work at this point would have been left in so untidy a condition with an irregular edge and a poor joint between itself and the hood mould of the arch.[22] It seems, therefore, from the available evidence, that the alteration to the doorway took place subsequent to the building of the church.

One further point needs to be noted: The pilasters flanking the south doorway are 19in. wide. At doorway level the pilaster surface is extended to the outer order of the doorway opening. It might be that the whole wall between the two pilasters was strengthened to support the heavy tympanum unit, or else that the original south doorway was built more substantially either to emphasise its importance or else to support an earlier lintel or tympanum.

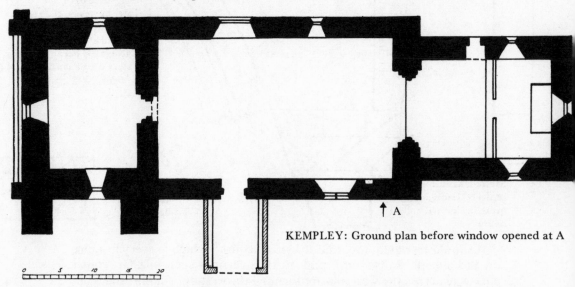

↑ A

KEMPLEY: Ground plan before window opened at A

0   5   10   15   20

(By Courtesy of the Bristol and Gloucestershire Archaeological Society)

It seems clear from these observations, and from the fact that the quality and variety of the carving upon the south doorway is in advance of all other Anglo-Norman work in the church, that there are in Dymock Church two quite distinct stages in the development of the local sculpture. The first is represented by the string course motifs, the heads of the blind arcading with the cushion capitals and patterned tympana and, finally, the small pairs of confronted volutes on the remaining capitals of the central tower block and the spur and scale motifs on the bases of these nook shafts and those on the broken responds further east. The second stage is represented by the tympanum, arch and the capitals of the south doorway. The reason for including the capitals in the second stage will be dealt with in the next section, in which the sculpture in St. Mary's Church, Kempley, will be considered. It would be convenient, however, at this point to make one observation. It is clear, when comparing these Dymock capitals and that of the pillar piscina at Preston, that the Dymock motif is a stylised version of the Preston example, and that, ultimately, they are derived from a common source. The change in the technique of the handling of this design and the obvious advance in workmanship would suggest a difference in date comparable with that between the two sculptural phases at Dymock. This would appear to make the Preston capital and the earlier carving at Dymock approximately coeval.

Kempley (St. Mary)

Kempley's original plan of aisle-less nave and rectangular chancel — the latter narrower than the former — was a design common in the Saxon period, e.g., Escomb and Odda's Chapel, Deerhurst, and continued to be used for many smaller parish churches well into the Norman era.

The stone barrel vault of the Kempley chancel is plain and of one piece. It is built of rubble of some thickness and contains stones of considerable size. The Romans introduced the technique into this country, and it was used in the construction of church crypts during the 7th to 11th centuries in a number of countries, among them France, Germany, Italy and Spain.[23]

The only example of barrel vaulting in masonry above ground level surviving in this country from the pre-Conquest period is found at Monkwearmouth. Sir Alfred Clapham stated that its use in the post-Conquest period was as infrequent in England as it was in Normandy.[24] The examples given are in cloister, porch and crypt, except in St. John's Chapel in the Tower of London (1080) and in Kempley parish church, but he does not suggest any reason for Kempley's unique position. It is possible that other parish churches once possessed this feature, but that in the course of rebuilding and alterations at later periods all traces of the barrel vaulting have been lost.[25]

Although not relevant to this study a brief note concerning Kempley's modern church, in view of its place in the Arts and Crafts Movement, should be included.

St. Edward's Church was built in 1903 by Mr. Randall Wells who, at the time he was approached by Earl Beauchamp, then the patron of Kempley, was a pupil[26] of Professor Lethaby, and engaged upon building the new church at Brockhampton near Ross-on-Wye. The influence of the master upon the pupil is obvious from even a glance at the two churches, an influence that is more marked upon closer inspection. Randall Well's passion for the 'local touch' and the unusual is seen at full flood at St. Edward's. The red Forest sandstone was used throughout and the timber for the roof was felled, trimmed and put in green from the Cockshoot Wood, Dymock. The Kempley blacksmith, a carpenter turned stone-carver from Dymock, and two Cotswold craftsmen were employed for the ironwork, stone-carving, and rood beam and furniture (candelabra, candlesticks, lectern etc.), but a ship's figure-head carver from London was imported to do the three rood figures. St. Edward's has rightly been termed a museum of local craftsmanship.

At Kempley six windows retain much of their early outline, but only four can help materially in the assessment of the building's date. These are the two narrow lights on the north (chancel and nave) and the two in the east wall. The former pair are similar in character and undoubtedly form part of the original building. As will be seen from the measurements of both windows[27] and from the photograph of the chancel north light (Plate 45B), there is a definite outer side splay in each case. The depth is approximately 4⅛in. Window splays of a similar design, if not of quite so pronounced a depth, are found in several local churches generally attributed to the 12th century.[28] The windows of the east end (Plate 46D) differ greatly in size and design. The top one, the loft light, approximates to those of the north wall. The chancel east window is a typical Norman light of its size, and has a plain nook shaft running right round the opening from two bulbous bases.

A closer inspection shows that the foot of this window is formed by three stones, and that the middle one (approximately 17½in. long) is bevelled at its centre for 13in. along its top edge, and, obviously, is a re-used sill stone (Plate 45C). The length of this stone is almost identical with those forming the sills of the narrow lights in the north wall, which also are cut away in a bevel at the centre. Might it have been that an earlier east window, coeval with and similar to the existing north windows, was enlarged soon after the church was built, still early in the Norman era, and that the original sill was re-used — perhaps not even moved?

Inside, too, alterations to the east window are suggested. The plaster face measurements are comparable with those of the window north and south, but the splays are steeper, as though they have been cut back, and a plain nook shaft with bulbous bases, similar to, but larger than, the outside set, has been let in to the wall, and borders the whole opening. The angle of the soffit, too, has been changed. It has been suggested that the East window was enlarged at a date well after the Anglo-Norman period, and that the external nook shaft is a 17th-or 18th-century imitation. Outside there is no supporting evidence for this view. The condition and nature of the stone of the nook shaft and bases are comparable with those of the ashlar blocks of the quoins and whole corner formation of the east wall. The carving has not the sharp edge definition that would have been expected had this very durable and compact sandstone been cut or re-cut as recently as the 17th or 18th century. This, in itself, would seem almost conclusive evidence of an early date for the alteration. Inside the chancel the evidence at first appears to be against an early alteration. From a height of approximately four feet the entire surface of the walls and vault retains its 12th-century fresco decoration. These paintings were whitewashed over in all probability at the time of the Reformation.[29] In 1872 they were discovered and cleaned.[30] The scheme of the paintings, the Majesty, is almost complete and is in a remarkable state of preservation. The paintings appear to contribute evidence of some importance on the matter of the alteration to the east window. The splayed sides and soffit of this window have been cut back since the original opening was made. These surfaces have been replastered at least once — perhaps more often, and today only a narrow fringe of frescoed plaster remains, showing the same colour combination and pattern as is seen in the splay of the north window and on the soffit of the south window. At first this may appear to be conclusive evidence of post-Reformation renovation, for if it had been pre-Reformation the whole splayed surface would undoubtedly have been re-painted.

Opposed to this argument, however, stand the following facts which appear to weigh heavily against the idea:

1 The nook shaft and bulbous bases on the inside obviously form part of the plan and scheme for the chancel at the time when the frescoes were painted: for the intact shaft to the south is taken as the boundary for the painted niche which surrounds the prelate — a thing inconceivable if the shaft had either been inserted or cut out at a time when the paintings were covered up and, presumably, unknown.

2 The shaft on the north side and part of its extension bordering the soffit have been damaged or destroyed and a plaster repair effected. Had this happened in pre-Reformation times, before the paintings had been covered over, it is probable that it would have been repaired or replaced in stone and any fresco damage made good.

3 The repair to the shaft and the damage to the frescoed splays must then have been of a post-Reformation date — this again seems possibly to support the 17th-or 18th-century date for the enlarging of the east window.

It is known that soon after 1631 a large and imposing monument was erected on the east wall between the east window and north wall. The monument, it is clear, caused the destruction of the plaster surface of that area. It may well have been responsible (through accident or intention makes no difference) for the damage to the nook shaft and plaster of the side of the splay and soffit. What is more natural than that the plasterer and mason, having caused such havoc, should have replaced almost the entire splayed area? It would appear that an explanation for the repairs and alteration to the east window splays must be sought along these lines.

4 A 17th or 18th-century mason and plasterer employed on opening up the east window would have cut back completely the sides and soffit. This would have resulted in the destruction of all plaster work of splays and soffit, and so have eliminated the obvious, ugly and uneven 'joint' and change in direction of the soffit plaster surface of this window.

The destruction and renewing of the plaster of splays and soffit probably are events of differing dates, with the latter taking place possibly even as late as the 19th century. The subsidence of the east end (whenever this occurred) may well have necessitated these repairs, or again (perhaps the most likely explanation) the repairs to the inside of the window could have taken place during the 1872 restoration. The crudeness of these repairs to the pillar and the roughness of the plaster joint are comparable with the untidy workmanship displayed in the repairs to the centre of the chancel vault.[31] Consequently, it would appear that on balance, the available evidence upholds the suggestion that the form of the east window was altered in the 12th century and that its inner surfaces were changed as the result of damage in 1872. All this lends support to the belief that at Kempley, as at Dymock, a two-stage development for the building within the Anglo-Norman period is probable.

The sculptured pieces within St. Mary's, Kempley, apart from the bulbous bases of the east window and a loose cross head, now pinned to the south wall of the vestry, are confined to the chancel arch and the south and west doorways; these have been dated as late as the third quarter of the 12th century and as early as the close of the 11th.

The cross head (Plate 53A) was found during the under pinning of the tower in 1912. The lower part of the shaft is shaped and rough, indicating that it had been fixed into masonry. Its height, or lack of it, suggests that it was not part of a standing cross; but rather the ridge cross of a building. It seems likely that, originally, it graced the west end of the nave roof, and that when the west tower was built in the 13th century the cross was removed, thrown down into the foundations being prepared, and finally was rescued in 1912. A somewhat similar but much weathered example is mounted at the east end of the chancel roof. The low relief of the carved cross and the broadened ends of the arms and head suggest native rather than Norman influence.

The more elementary carving is confined to the loose cross head, the original west doorway[32] and the capitals of the outer order of the chancel arch on the east side. These, by themselves, contribute little in the way of reliable dating evidence.

The south doorway enrichment is much more extensive. The hood mould shelters an arch with a double chevron pattern, while the tympanum motif — popularly termed the Tree of Life — is under a semi-circular roll and hollow mould and a double row of pellets (Plate 19C). The tympanum is similar to that at Dymock, and is, undoubtedly, from a common workshop, and could well have been the work of the same mason. The capitals are of a simple single scalloped pattern with the double curve carried down to the necking band in a semi-cone and having a dart in the angles between the cones. From the necking band rise pairs of small confronted volutes (Plate 32B). There are, as has been stated,[33] two features which call for comment. In the first place dividing each pair of volutes is a 'tau' or step motif with its arm resting upon the volute tops. The second feature is a triangular member which joins together the tails of the volutes backing upon each other. These paired volutes are, undoubtedly, a developed form of those upon the capitals of the nook shafts surviving in the central tower block at Dymock (Plate 32A), and represent a second stage in the evolution of the basic motif. It is possible that a period of some 20 to 25 years may separate the Dymock and Kempley examples. The paired confronted volutes at Dymock are bold, but crude in workmanship, and would be in keeping with the general character of carving in the early Anglo-Norman period. At Kempley a change of some magnitude has taken place. The lines are more flowing and the curves of the volute and tail are carved with a skill lacking in the execution of the Dymock examples. In addition, the introduction of the new features, especially the 'tau' or step motif, may indicate the revival of pre-Conquest influences and the re-introduction of such motifs as the step pattern. This latter motif, as has been stated, is employed locally in a large number of churches and in varying ways.[34]

The chancel arch of two orders is enriched with considerable carving which is, however, simple yet dexterous.

The inner order, sparsely decorated, is square in section and has upon its west face a hollow mould above a single band of sunken star motif. The motif partitions are oblong and match those upon the inner order at Pauntley and the earlier arch (c.1090) over the vestry doorway of Ely Cathedral. The east face of the Kempley arch is enriched with 10 roundels painted mainly in ochre (Plate 37B).

The outer order, on its west face, has a saw-toothed edge and single chevron pattern surmounted by a plain hood similar to those of both the west and south doorways. The sculpture of the whole west face of the arch retains much of its medieval painted decoration. The east face of the outer order is decorated in several colours, with a continuous step pattern in pyramid. The capitals of the archway merit careful study. The circular moulded members of the bases, with plain spur projections, rest upon two staged plinths of which the upper is bevelled. The shafts, as in almost every instance in the churches of the Dymock group, have no sculptural decoration.[35]

The capitals of the chancel arch are of great interest. Those of the outer order on the chancel side are of a plain cushion pattern and have not the finish of the other capitals. They are comparable with those of the west doorway (Plate 53C). There is, carved upon the east face of the chancel arch between the south capital and the south wall, and on a level with the capital, a very crude incised cross (Plate 53B). This may well be an original consecration cross. The west capitals of the outer order have scalloped bells with darts between, and a reversed scale or flat-leafed form (Plate 29B) — unlike the normal, outward curved design found both in classical or medieval sculpture — that fringe the neck of the shafts. The capitals of the inner order have upon their faces the stepped volute characteristic of the Dymock group of sculpture (Plate 29B). From the necking of the shafts of these capitals rise the same leaf forms, like scales reversed, carved upon the scalloped capitals of the outer order, and also upon most of the 'Dymock' large type capitals. The central leaf on the south and north faces has springing from it a long spear-head shaped leaf extending to the abacus and separating the two groups of volutes. The volutes are typical of the Dymock group; the three volute coils of each side of the corner spring from the leaf pattern above the necking band.[36] The first loses itself at the top of the capital. The second band bends round and over, and links up with the corresponding coil on other face to form the corner and the stepped pattern below. The third coil makes two and a half circles within itself. The whole motif creates the impression of a ram's head with stepped tongue protruding from the mouth. These Kempley capitals, although parallel in design to those at the south doorway in Dymock, are executed in a more convex form. The more bulbous nature of the Kempley design could suggest a definite departure from the earlier technique, representing either a slightly later date, or else the presence of a second mason in the local workshop — one not versed in native tradition or one more willing to accept Norman design.

Another explanation, which supports equally well the over-all two-stage development theory, may be nearer the truth. It is noticeable that whereas there are a number of closely-related examples of this type of capital with large volute and stepped tongue motif within the Dymock group,[37] two only are completely flat, giving the full low relief of Saxon cross technique. These are at Dymock and Pauntley, and both enrich south doorways. It is clear that the tympanum and arch over the Dymock south doorway were not part of the original building.[38] It is possible that, initially, the south doorway at Dymock had plain jambs, and that when the present tympanum and arch were introduced the capitals, shafts and bases were carved *in situ* from the jambs. It has been shown that at Dymock the volute face and point, the necking band and the base are all in one vertical plane.[39]

This would appear to confirm the suggestion that the Dymock south doorway volutes were carved upon existing plain jambs, and it would seem reasonable to suppose that they are contemporary with the tympanum and arch above them.

All this leads to the belief that both at Dymock and Kempley a two-stage development took place, i.e. that at Dymock a four-chambered apsidal church with simple sculpture, for example the string course, the blind arcading and the surviving capitals of the central tower, was later enriched by additional carving such as that of the south doorway, and that at Kempley a plain two-chambered building with a narrow east window was rebuilt or 'modernised' and enriched with more carving at approximately the time of the Dymock alterations (*c.*1110-25).

Newnham-upon-Severn Church (St. Peter).
The fourth church to be examined, Newnham, contains several interesting loose fragments of sculpture. Some of the motifs employed are those characteristics of the Dymock group, and may help to establish a third stage in its evolution.

A church at Newnham was first mentioned in 1016.[40] Another was said to have been re-built in *c*.1380.[41] It was rebuilt again in 1874/5. Finally in 1881 fire destroyed this church. A small Norman window frame or niche (with much chevron work) (Plate 46A) — now built into the wall high above the present north door of the nave — and several damaged stones (mainly capitals) are all that remain of the medieval church of which the Gloucestershire historian, the Rev. Thomas Rudge, wrote: 'The arch leading to the chancel shows considerable antiquity, being in the early Norman style, pointed and ornamented with zig-zag mouldings. The more ancient building . . . stood, according to tradition, at Nabb's End, but, being undermined by the water, was taken down . . '.[42] In a note on page 388 he adds: 'it is possible that the Norman arch leading to the chancel of this present building might have been preserved at the demolition of the first and re-erected in the second'. Fortunately, as mentioned above, the enrichment upon four of these stones[43] is so strikingly similar to that at Dymock and Kempley that there can be little doubt that the sculpture is closely related. There are, however, modifications of design which suggest that the Newnham examples are later than their counterparts at Kempley.

On the tympanum, although it is badly mutilated, can be seen the characteristic tree or archaic moth-like motif of the Dymock sculptural group. It is not really possible, because of the damaged condition, to say whether there is any advance in style or ornamentation. It would appear not to be the case (Plate 20A). The second stone is a capital from a doorway or the outer order of an archway. Here the whole design is based upon that found on the capitals of the central tower at Dymock Church and of the south doorway at Kempley, but is more ornately carved (Plate 32C). The capital is divided, as at Kempley, on each face, into two cones. The neck ring, however, is of a double cable pattern. The small confronted volutes, which follow so obviously the Kempley design, are more elaborately carved. The pronounced cursive treatment of the motif, especially of the 'T' and triangular members,[44] would suggest a third stage in the development of the local sculptural design and ornament, or else that the Newnham example was the work of a more ambitious sculptor.

The third loose stone is a capital which came from an archway[45] — the inner order if the archway was of multiple design. It is carved upon three faces, the centre one having twice the area of decoration of the others. The motifs are familiar, i.e. the straight leaf or inverted scale rising from the necking band and the large volute with stepped tongue.[46] These last, as at Kempley, are bulbous and protrude beyond the neck.

The remaining capital came, as did the first, from a doorway or the outer order of an archway, and is very badly damaged. There is, however, an area of carving intact on one face. Sufficient of the design has survived (Plate 47B) to suggest that it is based either upon the leaf group of the above-mentioned tympanum immediately above and below the bare cross or triple bud feature,[47] or else that it forms the tail of some mythological creature (e.g. the Wessex wyvern) or bird (e.g. the phoenix). I incline to the latter view. There is at Newnham, whichever interpretation is accepted (foliage or figure design), a significant addition. The curled leaf (or tail) design issues not from a plain branch. Instead the branch (or the latter portion of the tail, if a wyvern) has the appearance of ribbon, and is pelleted in the manner frequently found in Anglo-Norman ornamentation of the second and third quarters of the 12th century, e.g. the vine stems on the Kilpeck tympanum.

It would seem from the evidence at Newnham of the developed state of the small paired volute design, and from the appearance of pelleted ribbon and figure motifs, that an advance in technique and an extension of sculpture range is indicated. This could suggest that these features should be dated some 20-25 years later than the second sculptural stage at Dymock and Kempley. It must be borne in mind, however, that the Newnham tympanum and the large double capital from an archway appear to show no such advance. Consequently a date some 10-20 years after the work at Dymock and Kempley might be more realistic.

The remaining survivals from Newnham's Anglo-Norman church are the moulded and spurred base of a pillar, the frame or niche already mentioned and a font.

The niche is squat, and its sides and arch are enriched with much chevron carving. It has the appearance of mid-12th-century work.

The font at Newnham, with its arcaded bowl (Plate 43C), is a most interesting specimen, and forms part of a small local group which are so similar that, probably, they came from a single workshop. It is usually held that there are four fonts in this group, i.e. Newnham, Mitcheldean[44] and Rendcombe in Gloucestershire, and the font in Hereford cathedral. It is as well to remember that Mitcheldean and Newnham[49] formed part of the medieval diocese of Hereford. Mr. Marshall included in this group the stone shaft section of the Burghill font. This shaft, or perhaps discarded font, [50] is surrounded by a series of arcades in each of which is carved an apostle. Although smaller than the established fonts of this design the Burghill shaft is treated in the same manner both in regard to figure and ornamental enrichments, which suggest that Mr. Marshall may well be right in attributing the Burghill shaft to the hand that carved the fonts of Newnham, Mitcheldean, Rendcombe and Hereford.

The Newnham font figures of the Apostles are somewhat rudely worked. The heads are bare, but beards and moustaches are depicted, and eucharistic vestments clothe the figures whose symbols — apart from St. Peter and his key — it is not really possible to identify. All carry books[51] in their hands. The pillars or responds of the arcading and the borders top and bottom are enriched with a variety of Anglo-Norman motifs such as foliage, chevron, sunken star and pelleted ribbon. Mr. Marshall dates the Hereford Cathedral font between 1140 and 1145;[52] consequently that may also be the approximate date of the Newnham font. This would seem to be an acceptable figure, whether the font is contemporary with the loose capitals and other fragments within the church, or whether it is a somewhat later addition. It is of interest to notice that the Hereford font has supporting beasts which are somewhat similar in appearance to those on the font at Castle Frome. This last font is one of the outstanding works of the Herefordshire School of Sculpture. It is possible that the Hereford Cathedral font, with its beasts' heads, representing a date prior to that of the font at Castle Frome, before, as Professor Zarnecki has established,[53] the pilgrimage of Oliver de Merlimond to Santiago de Compostela caused a revolution in Herefordshire sculptural design and technique and in the sources of patronage of the arts,[54] which brought into being the Herefordshire School of Sculpture.

Summary

It would appear from the surviving examples of the common motifs employed in the churches of Preston, Dymock, Kempley and Newnham-on-Severn that:

(a) a development and growing maturity may be observed;

(b) by relating the examples one to another and to the other local contemporary sculpture a possible date bracket and chronological order is suggested.

Upon the strength of these hypotheses an attempt will be made in chapter eight to expand the chronological table by incorporating the works of sculpture which will be discussed in chapter seven, and also the tentative inclusion of other buildings containing sculpture or building techniques which have been briefly mentioned in earlier chapters.

NOTES

1. R.C.H.M. (Herefs.), vol. 3, p.32.
2. e.g. Dymock, pp.24-31, Moccas pp.60-63.
3. The pillar piscina first appeared, it is believed, early in the Norman period. The only other surviving local example which may possibly be contemporary with the Preston capital is in St. Mary's Church, Monmouth.

4. The nave side jamb edges of the s. transept have, in places, been bevelled.
5. The scars where the buttresses and archway on the w. side of the central tower block have been removed are still visible. A faculty (dated 14 Sept. 1727 and in the Gloucester City library) gives details of the petition for the removal of these, and also of a 'pillar adjoining the N. Isle'. This latter might mean that the main arch leading to the n. transept had within it two recessed arches supported by a central pillar.
6. Sir Alfred Clapham, addressing the Bristol and Gloucestershire Archaeological Society in Dymock Church, 6 May 1950.
7. C.N.F.C. *Proceedings,* vol. 2, pt.1, pp.41-48 and plans.
8. Clapham (b), p.101.
9. F.H. Fairweather, *Aisleless Apsidal Churches of Great Britain,* (Colchester, 1933).
10. A.W. Crawley-Boevey, *The Cartulary and Historical Notes of the Cistercian Abbey of Flaxley,* (Exeter, 1887), p.159.
11.

	Position of Dymock in Gloucestershire	
	excluding 6 combined	including
	manors	all
Hidage Value	12th	13th
Area under cultivation	3rd	6th
Male population	6th	10th

12. Cf. similar arcading at Deerhurst (Glos.) and Bradford-on-Avon (Wilts.), Saxon, and Milborne Port (Som.) *c.*1070, Anglo-Norman.
13. The church of Azay-le-Rideau (Indre-et-Loire) has this pattern in its w. wall (Joseph Gantner & Marcel Pobe, *Romanesque Art in France,* (English trans. 1956), Plate 210). This work is attributed (Gantner, *op.cit,* p.71) to the early 11th century.
14. The base on the s. side has been badly damaged and all evidence for or against a spur motif has been destroyed.
15. Morienval (Oise) - Gantner, *op.cit.,* Plate 236.
16. e.g. Leominster and Rowlstone (Plate 33A-C). This motif is also carved upon an impost of the chancel arch at Cusop. R.C.H.M. (Herefs.), vol.1, Plate 8.
17. Four miles from Dymock.
18. See above, pp. 16-17.
19. The w. wall of the Lady Chapel or s. transept hinders observation on the e. side of the doorway.
20. Plate 58A-D shows, in detail, the points mentioned.
21. The pairs differ from each other.
22. On the n. wall (internal) of the chancel the string course is brought up to the broken respond of the arch; there it ends neatly, and no attempt is made to allow it ot over-ride the respond.
23. It was the most usual roofing form in the style of architecture known as the First-Romanesque.
24. Clapham (b), p.59.
25. Mention must be made, too, of the barrel vault of the crypt in Duntisbourne Rous Church near Cirencester. Here the church has been built into the hillside, and the crypt is, very largely, above ground.
26. Perhaps Clerk of Works.
27. See below p.49.
28. The windows of the three lowest stages of Churcham w. tower, on its s. face, have splays of almost the same depth. No other windows of local parish churches of the Anglo-Norman period have comparable splays.

29. J.E. Gethyn-Jones, *St. Mary's Church, Kempley and its Paintings*, (Gloucs., 1961), vol.1, pp.13-15. (Hereafter cited as Gethyn-Jones (b).)

30. *Ibid.,* pp.16-19.

31. *Ibid.,* Plate IV, showing vault before work began in 1956.

32. 7ft. 6¾in. by 2ft. 10in. This is made up of cushion capitals, plain tympanum (Plate 35C) enriched by hollow hood mould, a single half-roll and hollow mould, and moulded bases with crude spur motif.

33. See above, p.18.

34. See above, p.15-16. e.g. Hereford Cathedral and Eldersfield (capitals), St. Mary's Monmouth (string course), Stoke Orchard (font), Deerhurst (figure), Hatfield and Much Dewchurch (lintels).

35. The only exception is at Yatton, Herefordshire, where the inner nook shaft (E.) has enrichment (Plate 42B), and p.44.

36. A carving of a winged beast upon a Roman table (2nd century), illustrated in G. Kowalozyk, *Decorative Sculpture,* (1927) with an introduction by A. Koster, Plate 106, could suggest a small leaf formation and the tall example could be identified as wing feathers.

37. e.g. Bridstow, Bulley, Churcham, Dymock, Fownhope, Newnham, Pauntley and Preston.

38. See above pp.27-30.

39. See above p.28.

40. Pershore Abbey Grant, see M.K. Woods, *Newnham-on-Severn. A Retrospect.* (Gloucs. 1912), p.57.

41. *Ibid.,* p.58-9. From the surviving Romanesque remains it is clear that there must have been a church built or rebuilt in the 12th century. It would be, presumably, this church which was rebuilt in 1380.

42. T. Rudge, *op.cit.,* vol.2, p.73.

43. Three capitals and a tympanum.

44. See above pp.18-19.

45. It came, in all probability, from the chancel arch.

46. The two corners are badly damaged, but a fragment of the step pattern can be seen on the one corner. It may be assumed, therefore, that the motif once existed on the other.

47. On the w. side of the Kempley tympanum and on the e. at Dymock.

48. The lower part only is original — B. and G. Arch. Soc. *Trans.,* vol.34, (1911), p.200.

49. Four miles apart.

50. For the full story, as far as it is known, see G. Marshall, *Fonts in Herefordshire,* vol.1 (1949), pp.15-18 and illus. 17. (Hereafter cited as Marshall (b)).

51. One book only is open.

52. Marshall (b), p.21.

53. G. Zarnecki, *Later English Romanesque Sculpture 1140-1210,* (1953), pp.9-15. (Hereafter cited as Zarnecki (c).)

54. There were powerful and generous patrons of church buildings in Herefordshire before this date, e.g. Walter and Hugh de Laci.

Chapter 7

Further Examples
of the Dymock Group of Sculpture

In addition to Dymock, Kempley, Newnham and Preston there are a number of churches in Gloucestershire, west of the Severn, and Herefordshire, and one each in Shropshire and Worcestershire (see location map) which contain examples of the sculpture characteristic of the Dymock group. Several of these churches, e.g. Bridstow and High Ercall, have been so altered by rebuilding or restoration that little of the original Anglo-Norman structure has survived. At High Ercall, for example, a tympanum alone (with tree motif) remains to confirm the existence of a church in that village before the mid-12th century.

There are also in the area being considered a few other churches which, although they possess no recognisable sculpture of the Dymock group, contain other features, such as string courses, which are closely paralleled by examples in the main body of churches within the Dymock group. It is possible that some connection or relationship existed between the established corpus of sculpture and these other features. A study of these additional works might result in an extension of the dating time-table and a broadening of the motif catalogue within the Dymock group of sculpture.

In this chapter, as with the previous one, the large voluted capitals will be considered first. The tympana motifs will next be examined. The string courses and the stepped motifs — those divorced from the volute — will then be studied, and an attempt will be made (if it appears likely that certain of them come within the survey of the Dymock sculptural group) to place them chronologically in relation to the main body of sculpture. Finally the employment of the basic 'Dymock' motifs in a more advanced and elaborate form will be suggested.

There are, in addition to the churches already considered in chapter 6,[1] six others,[2] possessing one or more of the characteristic stepped voluted capitals. These latter will be dealt with in the following order: Bridstow and Yatton, Fownhope, Bulley and Churcham, and, finally Pauntley.

Bridstow Church (St. Bridget) and Yatton Church (dedication not known)

Bridstow and Yatton are about six miles apart. Their sculptural enrichments have certain points in common. The craftsmanship at Bridstow, however, is superior to that at Yatton.

Bridstow, as such, is not mentioned in Domesday, but both in that Survey and in the Herefordshire Domesday (Balliol College MS. 350) of nearly a century later, it would appear to have been included in Clive[3] with its Berewick called Wilton, where in the later MS. a church and a priest are recorded as attached to the Abbey of Cormeilles. The de Laci family also held local interests. Yatton is a part of Much Marcle, and in Domesday[4] the entry relating to the latter place records that Cormeilles had a church and a priest at Marcle. The font alone in the present Marcle Church is of a pre-1150 date.

In view of these common interests in Bridstow and Marcle during the Norman period, and the proximity of these places to one another, it is perhaps less surprising to find sculptural affinities between Bridstow and the Marcle chapelry of Yatton in the 12th century.

The chancel arch is the only section of the Bridstow Church which has survived from its Anglo-Norman foundation. The arch is of two orders, the capitals of which are enriched with foliage motifs. Those on the south side (respond and outer order west) have carved upon them the large volutes with stepped tongues (Plate 29A) characteristic of the Dymock group. They are of the convex type found locally, for example on the chancel arches at Kempley and Pauntley chancel arch and, loose, at Newnham. On the north side the respond capitals are decorated with what might be termed an inverted acanthus or anthemion motif, which at the south-west and south-east corners are linked by a triple cord or band, which, viewed from the front, resembles the nose-band of a bridle (Plate 42C). The capital of the outer order has upon its south and west faces respectively a four-pointed star within a circle and a five-leafed sprig. The latter motif is found in several churches in the Hereford diocese.[5] The four-pointed star is a design which was employed locally from early in the Anglo-Norman era, e.g. the Bredwardine group of lintels. Neither of these two motifs is reproduced at Yatton where the south doorway alone (except for a thin shaft, enriched with cable and twisted and pelleted ribbon pattern, re-used in a window frame) retains original sculpture. There the enrichment is extensive and varied.

The Yatton doorway is of three orders (Plate 21A). The innermost is square in section, with corbelled projections supporting the tympanum. These projections are enriched with chevron work running vertically. At Kilpeck — about 12 miles distant as the crow flies — this same pattern is used on the lintel supporting the tympanum.

The outer orders at Yatton have nook-shafts of which the inner one on the east side is enriched with the spiral pelleted ribbon work similar to that upon the re-used shaft in the south window frame. All four capitals of the shafts have carved ornamentation, while two bases are moulded, one of which has a spur projection. The middle order capitals are enriched with a bridle nose-band motif (Plate 42A & B) similar to that carved on the north respond capitals of the chancel arch at Bridstow. It is not a pattern which has survived in this particular form in any other local church, but a more elaborate example enriches a nave capital in St. Peter's church, Northampton.[6] At St. Peter's the bridle nose-band is pelleted, and although the carving on the capital is treated in a way comparable to that at Yatton, it is more advanced and detailed.

The outer order of the arch above the south doorway at Kilpeck is enriched with nine medallions with pelleted borders. The medallions are inhabited by birds, beasts and fishes, and linked by flat masks which have about them a suggestion of an ornate example of the Bridstow, Yatton and Northampton feature.

The motifs on the capitals of the outer order at Yatton differ: that on the east has a series of upward curved incised semi-circles, and two downward lines (Plate 42B), giving a cushion capital effect. The companion capital to the west has a volute with stepped motif. The volute springs from a wedge-shaped panel (Panel 42A), the point of which rests upon the necking band. From the point at which the volute line begins to curve over, a tendril springs out in a manner reminiscent of pre-Conquest running foliage. The step pattern is broader and more squat than the normal ones, e.g. at Bridstow, Dymock, Kempley and Pauntley. The only comparable examples are those on the capitals of the central window shafts in the third stage (south and north faces) of the central tower at Fownhope (Plate 30A and B).[7] The similarity is so marked that a common hand is suggested. It must be pointed out, however, that the workmanship at Yatton is cruder than that at Fownhope.

The absence of figure carving and the nature of the foliage[8] and geometrical designs on the Bridstow chancel arch suggest that this work cannot be dated earlier than the second stage of the sculptural development in the churches of Dymock and Kempley, i.e. c.1115-20.

The style, treatment and workmanship of the voluted capitals at Bridstow are so similar to those of the inner order capitals of the chancel arch at Kempley that a common hand may be presumed.

The employment upon the north capitals at Bridstow of motifs[9] not found at Dymock and Kempley[10] might imply that the Bridstow chancel arch, with its saltire and chevron enrichment and carved capitals, should be dated either at the commencement or end of the period 1115-20. The presence of the chevron work would support more readily the later date — perhaps 1120-25.[11]

Fownhope Church (St. Mary)

St. Mary's Church, Fownhope, consists of chancel, central tower South chapel and aisle and north porch. The tower is the only section of 12th-century date.[12] Built into the west wall of the nave, on the inside, is a mid-12th-century tympanum on which are carved two figures, and also the symbols of St. John and St. Mark and some interwoven foliage. The surviving Romanesque sculpture is limited to the re-set tympanum and certain carving contained within the tower. The tympanum is one of the more important products of the Herefordshire School of Sculpture and has been examined in detail by Professor Zarnecki in his 1951 thesis (pp.337-342), where he described the figures as those of the Virgin and Child. The Professor now suggests that they may represent two members of the Trinity with the Dove possibly carved upon a voussoir now lost. Dr. T.S.R. Boase appears to agree with the latter identification.[13] I concur.

The surviving 12th-century sculpture in the tower is confined to the west archway of the lowest stage, the round-headed twin lights of the third stage, the string courses dividing the stages and the coping band (with small heads at each corner) at the base of the spire.

The west archway carving has no special importance in this examination.

The twin lights in the east and west faces of the third stage of the tower at Fownhope have simple cushion capitals upon the central shaft. The shafts in the north and south faces have capitals enriched with volutes having stepped tongue motifs.[14] The shaft in the north face is shielded externally by the clock dial, while the mechanism inside the tower makes inspection and photographing of the capital difficult. It would appear, however, that the volute (Plate 30B) is similar to the corresponding capital upon the south face. (Plate 30A).

The capital in the south face is fully exposed, and it will be observed that the carved lines forming the volute spring not from a leaf or scale pattern but direct from the necking band, as in the case at Yatton. The smaller leaf motif is absent, and the place of the large central leaf (like a spear head), found at Bridstow, Dymock, Kempley, Newnham and Pauntley, is taken on the south face by a curved triangular wedge which is similar in appearance to the corresponding Preston feature. At Preston, however, the smaller leaves are present and a ramshead takes the place of the volute.

The north capital has the broad stepped volute, and is also scalloped. The two cones, with dart between them, can be seen on the east and west faces (Plate 30B) — the north face is covered by the clock dial. The north capital appears to have a better finish than that of the south capital. This is the only example within the Dymock group where the stepped volute is found upon a scalloped capital. The scallop and dart feature is somewhat similar to that upon the outer order capitals on the west face of the chancel arch at Kempley (Plate 29B) where, however, the small leaf motif is present.

The stepped motif at Fownhope is shallower and broader than in any other examples in the group, except that on the one capital of the south doorway at Yatton.

These facts present a considerable dating problem.

The similarity of treatment of the step motif at Yatton and Fownhope — as has been stated — is so marked that a common hand or inspiration may be assumed.[15] The absence at both places of the leaf pattern rising from the necking band supports this assumption.

The triangular wedge formed at the centre of each face of the Preston pillar piscina capital and that on the south face of the south shaft capital at Fownhope are alike, a fact which may have some relevance. It could be that the pillar piscina capital design at Preston followed closely a basic pattern.

Later, in the second decade of the 12th century perhaps, there could have emerged another workman of greater skill and imagination, a head-man maybe, whose influence, if not his hand, would appear to have been responsible for much of the work on the Bridstow chancel arch, the Dymock south doorway, the Kempley chancel arch and south doorway and Pauntley south doorway, and possibly also the Pauntley chancel arch. The attributing of the Pauntley chancel arch capitals to the sculptor who produced the mature capitals enumerated above is tentative, and will be discussed at greater length when Pauntley Church is examined.

Then, perhaps in the third or fourth decade of the 12th century, an apprentice or less skilled workman may have been responsible for such work as the Fownhope south window shaft capital and the Yatton south doorway.

An alternative explanation might be that Yatton Church and Fownhope tower are considerably earlier than the 'mid-12th century' date suggested by Sir Alfred Clapham.[16] This earlier date cannot be maintained when the chevron work of the string course is remembered, and when the similarity in appearance and style of the heads on the coping band at Fownhope with certain of the Kilpeck corbel table heads is considered.

Bulley Church (St. Michael and All Angels) and Churcham Church (St. Andrews).

There are at Bulley and Churcham examples of the stepped volute capitals. These, however, show variation among themselves and from the usual pattern found within the group.

The nave of Bulley Church has been altered very little. The chancel is modern.[17] All the surviving original features of the nave are of 12th-century appearance, and the diamond pattern of the chevron work on the outer order of the south doorway suggests a date towards the middle of that century.

The capitals at the south doorway are of the 'Dymock' type, but display differences of detail (Plate 31A and B). Both these capitals have five curved arms (instead of the usual three). Those of the West capital rise from leaves which are smaller and more numerous than those found at Bridstow, Dymock, Kempley, Newnham, Pauntley and Preston; those on the east capital spring direct from the necking band; cf Fownhope and Yatton. The west capital has a badly damaged corner, making it impossible to be certain of the full details of the volute, but a fragment of the step pattern has survived on the east face (Plate 31A). The east capital is intact. The volute is pendulous and, apart from its counterpart on the west side and the single example at Churcham (and these three differ in detail among themselves) is unlike any other capital within the group. Beneath the volute to the east are confronted step patterns set vertically (Plate 31B). This vertically confronted double step pattern is not found elsewhere among the 'Dymock' type capitals.

The Churcham example of the stepped voluted capital is built into the outside of the south wall of the nave at a height of about 15 feet. There are some unattached voussoir and jamb stones (carved with simple roll or hollow mould) built in near it. These five stones, set almost as though they form part of a destroyed window frame, seem to be related.

The curve of the voussoirs would appear not to rule out the idea of a window frame. The chancel arch is large, and although Mr. Hobart Bird points out[18] that the archway has been repaired and includes much new material, sufficient has survived of the original work to make it reasonably certain that the capital never formed part of the chancel archway. The south doorway, too, has suffered much renewal[19] but retains sufficient original material to exclude the suggestion that this doorway once contained these now separated stones. The north doorway of the nave which Mr. Hobart Bird called 'modern' contains in the tympanum a few original stones[20] which, bearing in mind the Chepstow Castle tympanum, may well be contemporary with the lower stage of the tower, where the surviving small round-headed windows on the south side (Plate 45D) (with splays deeper than in any other local Anglo-Norman church excepting St. Mary's, Kempley)[21] suggest a date early in the post-Conquest period. If the capital being considered ever formed part of this north doorway it is probable that at first it was plain or cushion in design (as are the capitals of the south doorway and chancel arch) and that at a later date, within the first half of the 12th century, it received its present position, and that of the other worked stones in the same area, would have to be accounted for by suggesting that they were built into the south wall during the rebuilding programme following the devastating 19th-century fire.[22]

The similarity of treatment of the volute capitals at Bulley and the single example at Churcham (in spite of some variation of detail) is such that it may be assumed that they are contemporary and the work of the same mason.

It will be observed (Plate 31A-C) that none of these three capitals has any trace of either the triangular feature present on the Fownhope and Preston capitals, or of the spearhead-like central leaf of Bridstow and Dymock and elsewhere. It is possible that these three capitals at Bulley and Churcham were carved by a third member of the workshop staff. It will be recalled that the capital at Bulley, enriched with the vertically confronted stepped pattern (stalactite-stalagmite fashion — Plate 31B) has no parallel amongst the capitals of the Dymock group. The motif, however, is found locally in other settings, i.e: (1) Deerhurst — in stone on the base of the Saxon carvings of the Madonna (Plate 37A), and (2) Kempley — wall paintings (12th century) on the east face of the chancel arch (Plate 37B).

Pauntley Church (St. John the Evangelist)

The Anglo-Norman sculpture in Pauntley Church is confined to the south doorway and the chancel archway. It is the only church within the Dymock Group where the capitals at the south doorway and at the chancel archway are of the same basic stepped voluted design. Those of the south doorway are similar to the south doorway capitals at Dymock. On each of these capitals the enrichment is flat and incised, with no part of the capital protruding beyond the jamb face. It is possible that all these four capitals were carved *in situ*. The measurements, both vertical and horizontal, of the south faces of the Dymock and Pauntley examples are almost identical. There are, however, differences of detail. At Dymock, as has been stated, the design on the south and inner faces has three curved lines (Plate 28A) and the single tall leaf motif. At Pauntley the south faces have four curved lines and the inner faces three, while the tall leaf is omitted. In this respect, and in this respect only, the Pauntley capitals are nearer in design to the Bulley south doorway capitals than to those at Dymock.

The Pauntley tympanum, supported by the jambs of the plain inner order, has at its base a single row of four leafed rosettes within a circle. The curved border of the tympanum is enriched with a single row of pellets and a half-round mould. The central portion of the tympanum is carved with a scale pattern (Plate 56A) such as enriches the shaft bases of the south respond which marked, on the inside of the church, the commencement of the apse at Dymock (Plate 55B), and the font bowl at Llantwit Major (Glamorgan). The lands of this latter religious foundation were given by Robert Fitzhamon (died 1107) to the Benedictine Abbey of Tewkesbury[23] which he had founded. The Pauntley tympanum, however, has been damaged at some period, and portions of it have been renewed. At the east side the surrounding band of half-round mould and pellet extends upwards for approximately a foot. On the west side only a few inches of the original have survived. The renewed band, made up of voussoir-shaped sections, is enriched with the same motifs. The top third of the scaled central section of the tympanum has also been renewed. It is extraordinary that so much of the original solid tympanum, on its curved portion, should have been broken away and renewed. The condition of the surviving part of the tympanum and the uneven edges of the break do not suggest that weathering or general deterioration necessitated the renewal, but rather an accident. Had this accident taken place during the original building it would be reasonable to suppose that a completely new tympanum would have been inserted. Is it possible that the chevroned arch and billeted hood mould are later additions to the enrichment of the south doorway? Some such thought as this may have been in the mind of Mr. Keyser when he wrote that the Pauntley south 'doorway is a curious mixture of late and early Norman work'.[24]

The chancel archway, too, presents problems. The arch is composed of two orders and a substantial hood-mould. The inner order enrichment parallels the inner order at Kempley with an oblong sunken star motif and hollow mould. The outer order has a double row of chevron work.

The hood mould is plain. The east side of the chancel arch is plain, and square in section.[25] The abaci are extended outwards as a string course on the west face to the side walls (north and south). The abaci and their extensions (the string course), are enriched with an inverted battlements motif.

The three faces of the inner order capitals are all enriched with the stepped voluted motif. The curved lines are four in number as on the south face of both south doorway capitals. On the inner face of these chancel arch capitals the central tall leaf motif is carved, and it is from the sides of this leaf formation that the fourth curved line springs. This tall leaf is a poor copy of the example found at Bridstow, Dymock and Kempley.

The grotesque heads carved upon the capitals of the outer order of the chancel arch (Plate 29C) are not unlike the one upon the outer order capital of the south doorway at Kilpeck (Plate 21B). These Pauntley grotesques and the figure (if it is one) upon the damaged loose capital at Newnham[26] and the crude ramshead carved upon the loose capital at piscina capital from Preston[27] are among the few surviving examples of figure sculpture found in close relationship with the Dymock Group.

The grotesque capitals, their abaci and the string courses appear to be original. The carving upon the capitals and abaci of the inner order, however, is sharper and clearer than that upon the outer order and upon the string course. The broad leaf spurs on the base of the respond on the south side of the archway are badly worn. Those on the north are sharply defined and are undoubtedly renewals, as indeed appears to be the whole base unit. The condition of the capitals and the obvious renewing of the respond base on the north side could suggest that the inner capitals may also have been renewed. A comparison of the stone used in the jambs and arch of the archway into the 14th-century south chapel and that of the capitals and responds of the inner order of the chancel arch is interesting, and could suggest that some of these renewals — if any took place — may have occurred during the period of the building of the south chapel.

The chronological placing of the Pauntley Romanesque sculpture is not easy. The chancel archway — presuming that the capitals of the inner order are either original or reasonable copies of the original — must be placed in the second quarter of the 12th century, although the enrichment of the arch itself (and especially that upon the inner order, so like that at Kempley) could well be somewhat earlier. The sculpture upon the south doorway appears to be a little earlier in date than that of the chancel archway, except that upon the inner order of the arch itself. The absence of the tall leaf motif on the capitals of the south doorway and the presence of traces of a fourth curved line on the south face of both the capitals could suggest that either they are earlier in date than the chancel archway work, or that these capitals (south doorway and chancel archway) represent the work of two different workmen, the one less skilled than the other. The more advanced carving, with grotesque figures, seems to represent the closing period of the Dymock group of sculpture and its absorption or replacement by workshops where new techniques flourished and where the grotesque and human figure designs were used.

Summary

There are in Herefordshire and Gloucestershire, west of the Severn, nearly 30 tympana on which are carved geometric, foliage or figure enrichments. There are also a number of composite tympana, e.g. Hatfield, and others which are plain, e.g. Kempley (original west doorway), or enriched with the simplest or geometrical or moulded work, e.g. Ledbury, Dymock (north wall).

The tree or foliage tympanum motif is the one principally associated with the Dymock group of sculpture. Of these eight, the Dymock, Kempley and Newnham tympana are clearly the product of the same workshop. The designs on the Hereford Cathedral and Yatton tympana might well have relationship with the previous three, while the Kilpeck tympanum subject (the vine) may be a developed form of the same basic motif.[28]

In addition to these Herefordshire and West Gloucestershire tympana with the tree or foliage motif there are in Shropshire and Worcestershire examples which follow so closely the general pattern that some relationship with the Dymock group may be assumed.[29] There are others where weathering now makes identification difficult.[30] Finally, there is the Buildwas tympanum where the elaborate nature of the carving makes a connection with the Dymock group a matter of conjecture (Plate 21C).

The churches containing the tympana associated with the Dymock group of sculpture and their surviving Romanesque material have been tabulated in the catalogue section of this study, while the Dymock, Kempley and Newnham features have been discussed more fully in chapters five and six. Consequently it will be necessary here to deal only with the tympana themselves and with those sculptured motifs which have significance in the chronological analysis of the tympana. There are, as has been stated, five tympana[31] and a font (Bromyard) enriched with the characteristic tree or foliage motif.

Bromyard Font

The most primitive form of the six examples of this particular (tree) motif is that carved upon the Bromyard font. It is unwise to date a building by its furniture, e.g. font or piscina, which could be and sometimes were considerably later than the building which houses them. Occasionally the reverse is true, and survivals from a previous structure are incorporated into the fabric, or included in the furniture of newer buildings, e.g. the tympanum at High Ercall (Plate 19A), and the 12th-century lead font in Oxenhall (Plate 57B), where the tower is 14th-century and the nave and chancel are 19th-century.

Bromyard Church enjoyed collegiate status in pre-Conquest days,[32] and from the Domesday details[33] it would appear possible that this was maintained — perhaps in a modified form — into the late 11th century.[34]

It is suggested by the Domesday description that Bromyard was the centre of a large district community at that period.[35] Consequently it would be expected that some programme of church building (or re-building) would have been begun before the mid to late 12th century, which is the date given by Sir Alfred Clapham to the earliest surviving parts of the present building.[36]

The Bromyard font is divided into two zones, the lower having a flat zig-zag pattern, while the upper has foliage enrichment. Two-thirds of the upper zone has the running tendril-like motif characteristic of much work on pre-Conquest standing crosses and manuscript illumination. The remaining area of the upper zone is decorated with a simple version of the motif on the Dymock type of tympanum (Plate 20B). It will be observed that the figure is crudely formed and has not the elaboration nor the finish of the examples at Dymock, High Ercall, Kempley, Newnham or Rochford.

It is unlikely, had the font been contemporary with the mid to late 12th-century parts of the building, or had it been introduced at a later date, that the carving upon it would have displayed so primitive a standard of workmanship, bearing in mind the position of the church and the quality of the carving upon the surviving 12th-century work in it.

Sir Alfred Clapham, writing of the Peter stone and the cross built into the wall above the re-set south doorway of the nave, said: 'it is just possible' that they were 'of the pre-Conquest period'.[37] They may be, but it would seem that Sir Alfred felt that a post-Conquest date was more likely.

It is of interest to note that the same type of cross in relief, carved upon a squared stone of similar size to the Bromyard example, is let into the wall above the north doorway of the nave in the Saxon church of

Stanton Lacy (Shropshire) (Plate 4B) which is less than 20 miles from Bromyard. The only appreciable difference between the stones is that the Bromyard example is set within a circular recess (Plate 4A). The St. Peter at Bromyard appears to be close in style and treatment (remembering the difference in the nature of the stone) to some of the loose capitals in Hereford Cathedral, for which, if the evidence of the recently removed window tympanum is reliable[38] (Plate 18C), a late 11th-century date must be given. If this is so, then a late 11th or very early 12th century date for the Peter stone and the cross — and, I would suggest, the font also — would be acceptable. It would seem possible that these three features may have survived from an earlier church, which was replaced or rebuilt in the latter half of the 12th century.

High Ercall Tympanum

The High Ercall tympanum would appear to be the next example, chronologically, of the same tree or foliage motif.

The central feature is simple in design (Plate 19A), following more closely the palmette or anthemion (with the addition of the opposed bare branches terminating in cross-beads or bud formation) which would appear to have been the pattern from which all the local examples have been derived.

The decorative border of the High Ercall tympanum has a six-leafed rosette motif similar in some respects to those carved upon the lintels at Bredwardine, Letton and Willersley (Plate 13A-D). The examples of the Bredwardine group, although the treatment is the same, are more elaborately carved, for example the spaces between the leaves are decorated with (1) smaller rosettes (Letton) or (2) pellets (Bredwardine and Willersley). The individual rosettes at the latter places are enclosed within a double circle. These differences, which seem to suggest an earlier date for the High Ercall tympanum, could, however, be accounted for by the larger size of the motif of the Bredwardine group which would allow further enrichment.

This reading is supported by the fact that the more ornate Rochford tympanum, which forms part of a doorway where motifs are present that are indicative of a date no earlier than the second quarter of the 12th century, has a similar band of the rosette motif forming the border of the central design.

The Dymock and Kempley tympana enriched with the characteristic motif, are more elaborately carved than that at High Ercall. The volute design at the latter is confined to two small examples near the stem of the base of the tree-like figure. At Dymock and Kempley each of the three groups of leaves on either side of the central stem has a small volute curved within itself. Furthermore, the top two side groups of leaves are fanned out like the fragment of the pattern surviving upon the badly-damaged loose capital at Newnham (Plate 47B). At the latter case, however, the stem is pelleted. The borders both at Dymock and Kempley are enriched with two rows of pellets and a hollow mould.

The tympanum at Yatton near Kempley, with a crudely carved copy of the characteristic motif, also has a pelleted border. The pellet device was employed in pre-Conquest illuminations and in Anglo-Saxon sculpture, e.g. on the short cross piece of a pilaster above the north doorway of the nave in Stanton Lacy (Plate 4B), but only came into common use here in the West in ribbon decoration during the second and third quarters of the 12th century, e.g. The Kilpeck tympanum.

If the tympana at Dymock and Kempley may be dated c.1110-25,[39] the High Ercall example could, stylistically, be earlier. The simplicity of the design of the latter, and the border motif (in spite of its employment at Rochford), could suggest a date some few years before that of the Dymock or Kempley examples. These latter have been dealt with fully either above or on p.35. The Newnham tympanum, too, has been described (p.38) in as much detail as its damaged and uncleaned condition[40] allows. The foliage or tree motif appears to conform to the Dymock pattern, with volutes, fanned leaves and bare branches with cross or bud-heads. The date of the tympanum in view of the greater elaboration upon a loose capital at Newnham, of the small confronted volutes motif which enriches the nook shaft capitals of the south doorway at Kempley, and the pelleted stem of the foliage (or animals tail?[41]) on another damaged loose capital at Newnham, could well be later than the Dymock and Kempley examples. These, it has been suggested,[42] must be contemporary with the Kempley confronted volutes capitals.

Rochford Tympanum

Rochford Church (now in the diocese of Worcester)[43] is, basically, a two-chambered building with later additions. The three small Anglo-Norman windows have little or no splay on the outer side. The chancel arch, of two orders, is enriched with outward-facing chevron work. The North doorway, of three orders, is extensively decorated with a variety of motifs.

The tympanum above this doorway has carved upon it an interesting example of the foliage or tree motif characteristic of the Dymock group (Plate 20C). The general form is that found at Dymock, Kempley and Newnham, with a central stem crowned with a group of upright leaves. On either side of the stem, two-thirds of the distance up from the base, a bare branch with a cross or bud-head shoots out. Below these bare branches are groups of downward-curving leaves. The lowest leaf on each side forms a base volute. Thus far the Rochford features correspond with the previously mentioned tympana. There are, however, certain distinctive elements at Rochford which must be considered. In the first place there are tendrils, in the manner of the running foliage of earlier days, which shoot out from several of the curved leaves. Secondly, it should be noted that in the treatment of the leaves a difference may be observed. At Dymock, High Ercall, Kempley and Newnham the leaves are formed by hollow chisel-work suggestive of a chip-carving technique. At Rochford this method, although employed, is less pronounced.

The two orders of the arch above the tympanum are enriched with outward-facing chevron work.

Upon the abaci at this doorway are two types of interlacings (Plate 20C), while the four capitals are enriched with several forms of volutes. The design upon the capitals of the inner order is made up of four lines springing from a small leaf form which enriches the necking band. The volute itself is pendulous, and the whole effect is reminiscent of the Bulley south doorway capitals (Plate 31B).[44] There is a faint suggestion of a step formation below the west volute. It is unfortunate, for comparison's sake, that the protruding portion of the volute upon the west capital of the south doorway at Bulley has been broken off.

The outer order capitals of this north doorway at Rochford have voluted motifs which bear no close resemblance to any within the Dymock group of sculpture. The east capital is enriched on its east side with an additional foliage design.

The outward-facing chevron motif is usually taken to represent a mid 12th-century date, i.e. 1135-70.[45] The similarity of the Rochford inner order capitals with those at Bulley, and the foliage design upon the eastern outer order capital would agree with a date in the latter half of the second quarter of the 12th century, that is c.1140.

The tendrils upon the tympanum motif and the rosetted border, although seemingly inconsistent with this mid-century suggestion, could be accounted for by the known revival of pre-Conquest design and motifs at that period.

It would appear reasonable, considering the evidence, to place the Rochford tympanum later in date than those of Dymock, High Ercall, Kempley and Newnham.

Yatton Tympanum

The remaining tympanum of the Dymock group, Yatton, has been mentioned previously, and the motifs upon the outer orders of the south doorway in that chapel have been considered in relation to certain capitals at both Bridstow and Fownhope.[46] The Yatton tympanum has the hollow mould and double row of pellets seen on those at Dymock and Kempley. The central tree motif, however, is (when compared with the counterpart on the tympanum at Dymock, High Ercall, Kempley, Newnham and Rochford) extremely crude (Plate 21A), and would appear to be the work of a less competent craftsman copying the known local examples. This would suggest that its date must be after that of the Dymock and Kempley tympana. The treatment of the capitals and other carved areas is more developed and confident, and (as has been pointed out) shows a knowledge of motifs at Bridstow and Fownhope. These facts would support (for the whole doorway) a date well into the second quarter of the 12th century.

In addition to the tympanum tree motif, the large stepped volute and the small confronted volutes there are other features in certain churches of the Dymock group upon which comment should be made.

(a) String Course

The first of these is the string course at Dymock. It has been pointed out that there are upon the string course of the south walls of the south chancel, old tower block and nave, two distinct motifs. The top third of the outer face of the string course on the west walls is enriched with a small rectangular design containing a pair of shallow confronted triangles. The lower zone has carved upon it either an incised double diamond motif (it might almost be termed a confronted chevron pattern) or else cable work (Plate 35C and E). Considerably more of this string course is enriched with the first motif.

The short length of string course surviving inside the church (north wall) is similar to the cabled sections of the south wall, i.e. top zone with rectangular design and lower with the cable pattern. A single section is also built in (upside down) above the south-west window of the chancel.

It is clear that the string course formed part of the blind arcading design on the south wall of the chancel, and was an intended component of the shallow pilaster scheme of the old central tower block and nave. This leaves no doubt that it formed an integral part of the original church. It must be assumed, therefore, that it is of late 11th-century date.

The cabled sections (both external and internal) are in better condition than the lengths enriched with the double diamond motif. Some of the latter are very badly weathered. It seems possible that the cable moulded sections on the outside face of the south wall came from the inside of the church during some period of reconstruction, and were inserted in the external course to replace damaged or badly weathered sections.[47]

At Linton, about six miles south of Dymock, the earlier part of the church is the west end of the north wall of the nave.[48] On the north face of this wall, which now forms the south wall of the north aisle, is a string course (Plate 35A & B) upon which is carved the more common pattern at Dymock. Domesday records that Linton Church and its priest were held by the Abbey of Cormeilles.[49]

The Domesday Dymock entry mentioned a priest, and the Rev. C. S. Taylor postulates that this indicates that a church existed there at that time.[50] Mr. Taylor also draws attention to the fact that the manor of Newent passed to Cormeilles before 1074 when Earl Roger was deprived of his estates.[51]

An Inspeximus of King Henry II records that Cormeilles held the churches of Newent, Taynton, Pauntley and Dymock.[52] It is not known when Cormeilles became possessed of these churches, because most of the charters of that Abbey have disappeared.[53] It is reasonable to suggest, bearing in mind the similarity of string courses and also considering the Domesday entries, that a stone church existed at Linton by the end of the 11th century or early in the 12th-century.

(b) Stepped Pattern

The stepped pattern associated with large volutes is one of the characteristics of the Dymock group of sculpture, and is found in this combination at nine churches, all of which are situated within a 12 mile radius of Dymock. This same stepped pattern, divorced from the volute but still carved mainly upon capitals, can be seen in a number of other churches within a radius of 20 miles, e.g. Eldersfield, Hereford Cathedral, Beckford, Upleadon (all capitals), St. Mary's, Monmouth (string course), Stoke Orchard (font) and Deerhurst (base of wall figure).

There are two forms of the motif in Eldersfield. At the chancel arch the stepped pattern, in a pendent and embossed form, is carved within a sunken shield-shaped area upon the flat faces of the cushion capitals of the nook shafts (Plate 38A). The narrow faces of the abaci are enriched with an incised zig-zag pattern. The whole effect is plain but pleasing. The present south doorway (15th century) has been built asymmetrically within a damaged 12th-century doorway. The surviving nook shaft on the west side of the latter has a cushion capital with, as at the chancel arch, darts at the corner. The flat surface of the capital has the same sunken shield with central stepped pattern similar to those carved upon the chancel arch capitals. The doorway capital, however, has a further enrichment in the form of a five-leafed sprig conforming to the three stages of the stepped motif (Plate 38B). Above the capital is a large fragment of the earlier archway, the inner order of which is enriched with outward-facing chevron work, while the outer order (it is in reality a broad flat hood-mould) is decorated with an interwoven pelleted ribbon pattern suggestive of a mid 12th-century date.

It is possible that the south doorway arch enrichment was a subsequent addition to an earlier 12th-century doorway and that at that time the stepped pattern, carved in relief, was worked upon it and the leaf pattern added.

The stepped motif within a sunken panel is employed as a continuous pattern enriching the round capital of one of the nave pillars in Hereford Cathedral. The cathedral was consecrated, presumably by then completed, during the episcopate of Robert de Bethune (1131-1148).[54] Consequently it may be assumed that the work on the central pillars of the nave would have been finished by c.1140, possibly a little earlier. It must be remembered, however, that there has been some restoration of the moulded caps of these columns,[55] but it is probable that the original motifs would have been reproduced in something approaching their earlier form.

The stepped motif at St. Mary's, Monmouth, is incorporated in a string course upon the outside west wall of the north-west turret (Plate 34C). It is made up of a basic flat saw-edged or chevron pattern. On this triangular pattern is the stepped motif in low relief. Upon the latter is a shallow chevron block in which has been gouged a wedge-shaped figure. The church of St. Mary's, Monmouth, was consecrated by Harve le Breton,, Bishop of Bangor, in 1101.[56] Sir Alfred Clapham dated the first appearance of the chevron in England at between 1110 and 1120.[57] This statement suggests that the turrets (north and west) at the west end of the nave at St. Mary's on which are the string courses — the north as described above and the south with the more normal chevron pattern — were later additions, or else that the consecration was that of the chancel only.

The outer capital (eastern)[58] of the south doorway at Beckford has upon its two faces, and within a pelleted border, a double stepped pattern — one super-imposed upon the other (Plate 38C). A pear-shaped feature hangs from the lowest of the three divisions of the lower stepped motif.

The Stoke Orchard font bowl has plain intersecting arch enrichment in low relief, the columns of which have capitals and bases built up on the step principle (Plate 39A).[59] The flatness of the decoration suggests a date early in the 12th century rather than late. This would be consistent with the plain tympanum and doorway on the south and the chamfered abaci and simple sculptured capitals of the chancel arch.

The highly enriched capital of the nook shafts (eastern) at the north doorway in Upleadon has immediately below the abacus upon both faces a very small example of the step motif (Plate 39C). It is clear from its insignificant size and its remote position upon the capital that this motif had lost favour.

The figure carving upon the capital, the tympanum enrichment and the mask above the chancel arch (eastern face) (Plate 47A)[60] suggests that, chronologically, this is a very late example of the stepped motif, and its relegation was no doubt soon followed by its omission as a decorative feature.

Moccas Church

At this point, the evidence for the dating of Moccas Church can be considered. The church is a three-chambered building, consisting of rounded apse, chancel and nave. The walls, except for the sandstone dressings of the archways of the chancel and apse and the two nave doorways, are entirely composed of calcareous tufa. The tufa enrichment is limited almost entirely to the apse. Both the plinth and string course (external) of the apse are chamfered, as are also the imposts of the windows inside the apse. The rear arches of these three windows have chevron decoration. The dressings of the archways and the nave doorways are enriched with geometrical, foliage and animal motifs.

Professor N. Pevsner makes no comment as to the date of Moccas Church.[61]

Sir Alfred Clapham, when writing generally of the church, described it as of 'about the second quarter of the 12th century.[62] Later in the same account he terms the blocked North doorway of the nave as of 'an early to mid 12th-century date',[63] Sir Alfred did not relate the building nor its carving to any local group of architecture or sculpture.

Professor G. Zarnecki, however, suggested that if a comparison were made between 'the sculpture on the two doorways of Moccas Church in Herefordshire . .(and) . . the Bromyard Font' it would be 'evident that they should be included in the same group'.[64] Professor Zarnecki bases his opinion upon the similarity of the scroll work upon the tympana and the font, and says that they 'should be placed early in the second quarter of the 12th century'.[65]

It will be observed that there is a great measure of agreement between Sir Alfred Clapham and Professor G. Zarnecki as to the date of the sculpture in Moccas Church. In this respect I concur.

I submit, however, that a different interpretation of the evidence as to the date of the main body of the building is possible. Furthermore, a relationship between the Moccas tympana and capitals and the Dymock group of sculpture — of which the Bromyard font is an important feature — appears to me, on the evidence available, to be tenable only if a somewhat prolonged life for the workshop of the Dymock group of sculpture be accepted, and a grateful development of its style and the enlarging of its repertoire be recognised.

Sir Alfred Clapham pointed out that calcareous tufa is found only in restricted areas, e.g. Kent and Herefordshire. He stated that its employment in south-east England could be accepted as some evidence for an early date, but concluded by saying that in other areas the use of local tufa 'continued well on into the 12th century'.[66]

Tufa was widely used in Herefordshire during the early days of the Anglo-Norman period, e.g. at Blakemere, Bredwardine, Edvin Loach, Hatfield, Letton, Moccas, Monkland, Tedstone-Delamere, Tedstone Wafer and Wigmore. It will be noticed that of these Bredwardine, Edvin Loach, Hatfield, Letton, Monkland, Tedstone Wafer and Wigmore are accepted as of late 11th-century date.[67] In addition the possibility of a late 11th-century or even a pre-Conquest foundation in the case of Tedstone Delamere is not ruled out.

It is of interest, perhaps very relative, that tufa is incorporated into the tympana or the inclosing arches at Bredwardine, Edvin Loach, Hatfield, Letton, Moccas (both doorways), Tedstone Delamere (triangular strip label over the blocked north doorway) and Tedstone Wafer, while Monkland and Wigmore have no surviving original doorways.

It may not be without significance that three out of the four surviving doorways of the 11th-century churches of Bredwardine and Letton (these two parishes and that of Moccas adjoin) were altered early in the 12th century. The addition of enriched lintels over the north and south doorways of the nave at Bredwardine and over the south doorway at Letton is a fact accepted by Sir Alfred Clapham[68] and Professor G. Zarnecki.[69]

A similar course of events took place at Dymock in the first quarter of the 12th century when, it is evident, the tympanum and the surrounding chevroned arch were inserted above the south doorway.[70]

Is it possible that the Moccas doorways were also altered?

Blakemere, apart from Moccas, is the only one of the Herefordshire churches enumerated above which is not said to be of 11th-century date. It will be observed that Blakemere Church contains less tufa material than any of the others, where, indeed, tufa is extensively used. It seems strange that a church so completely constructed of tufa (except for certain archway and doorway dressings) should have been built at a time when the use of this material was far less common than had been the case in the 11th century.

It is probable, were it not for the dressings of the archways and doorways, that a 11th-century date would have been assigned to Moccas.

It will be noticed, upon close examination of the north and south doorways at Moccas, that there is a narrow concave band of tufa sandwiched between each tympanum and its enclosing chevroned arch (Plate 59A & B). This band is too narrow and insignificant to achieve any decorative effect. How can its presence be explained?

It will be seen also that in the north doorway tympanum recess there are two short lengths of voussoir-shaped moulded beading between the tufa strip and the tympanum (Plate 59A). These two stones are of sandstone of a much lighter colour than that of the tympanum. They also break into the tympanum in an ugly way. They 'sit', however, easily with the tufa, and conform naturally to the curve of that band. If a section of the tympanum at a later date had been damaged it is improbable that a repair would have been carried out with so ill-matching a colour and so differing a design.

These two stones, although considerably narrower, are similar in moulding and shape to those of the stone beading which encloses the composite 11th-century tympanum over the south doorway at Letton. There is no trace of similar moulding in Moccas.

Is it possible that Moccas is basically a late 11th-century church, and that at some time in the first half of the 12th century a desire was expressed to enrich and beautify the church as had already happened in the case of the neighbouring churches of Bredwardine and Letton?

Could it have been that an original north doorway tympanum at Moccas was a composite one, similar to that over the south doorway at Letton? If the new tympanum with scroll work and animal motif had arrived with a fragment either missing or so badly damaged that a proper repair could not be effected, is it beyond the bounds of possibility that the mason in charge retained the two sections of the original beading, trimming both them and the damaged tympanum so that a reasonable fit could be effected? The chancel and apse archways could have received enrichment at about the same period.

A recapitulation of the main facts and problems is now necessary.

a   It is strange that a three-chambered church should have been built almost entirely of tufa during the second quarter of the 12th century, a time when the use of this material, local evidence suggests, was less popular than in former years.

b   None of the other local churches in which tufa constitutes a major building material have any animated or whimsical carving upon their tympana. Bredwardine (south), Edvin Loach, Hatfield and

Letton (south) have composite tympana, while the Bredwardine (north), Letton (west) and Tedstone Wafer[71] tympana were plain.

c There is a concave tufa surround to the north and south tympanum —why?

d The moulded stones protruding into the north tympanum at Moccas raise the question — why?

That Moccas was a late 11th-century church which was altered and enriched subsequently would appear to be as reasonable an interpretation of the evidence as the generally accepted view. I would go further, and suggest that it is the more probable explanation.

NOTES

1. Dymock, Kempley, Newnham and Preston.
2. Bridstow, Bulley, Churcham, Fownhope, Pauntley and Yatton.
3. A tithing of Ross. See V.C.H., *Herefordshire,* vol.1, (1908), pp.322 (hereafter cited as V.C.H. (a)), a Balliol MS. No. 350, f.6.
4. V.C.H. (a), p.313.
5. e.g. the s. doorways at Bromyard and Upper Sapey.
6. Clapham (b), Plate 7. These nave capitals are dated 1160-70 by Clapham. Zarnecki, however, placed them at *c.*1150. This would appear to be a more acceptable date, bearing in mind the similarity of treatment and design with certain of the capitals in the crypt at Canterbury Cathedral and the closely-dated capitals here in the West, e.g. Leominster.
7. Fownhope is four miles from Yatton.
8. The absence of the pellet which enriches much of the ribbon features upon certain works of the Herefordshire School, e.g. Kilpeck tympanum, suggests that it is of a pre-Herefordshire School date.
9. Four-painted star, five-leafed sprig and inverted acanthus with bridle nose-band effect.
10. Newnham is not here included in view of the fragmented nature of the 12th-century survivals in that church.
11. Were it not for the chevron work a case might be made out for the earlier date.
12. R.C.H.M. (Herefs.), vol.2, p.80.
13. Boase, *op.cit.,* p.83; see also B.M. Harley MS. 603, f.l.
14. The carving on both capitals in confined to the outside face and part of the sides. The remaining surfaces (the inner face and part of the sides) have no enrichment.
15. Could the cruder work be that of a pupil?
16. R.C.H.M. (Herefs.), vol.2, pp.80 and 225.
17. R. Bigland, Garter King of Arms, in his *History of Gloucestershire,* (1786), said that 'Bulley is without aisle or chancel'.
18. W. Hobart Bird, *Old Gloucestershire Churches,* p.67. (Hereafter cited as Hobart Bird (a).)
19. The result, maybe, of the fire which gutted the nave and chancel in 1875.

20. Hobart Bird (a), p.67. The extensive renewal here may be due to damage received when the church was gutted by fire in 1875.
21. See above p.32.
22. No plans relating to this restoration and rebuilding have been traced.
23. C.J.O. Evans, *Glamorgan, its History and Topography,* (Cardiff, 1938), p.115.
24. C.E. Keyser, 'An Essay on the Norman Doorways in the County of Gloucester', in *Memorials of Old Gloucestershire,* (1911), p.162. (Hereafter cited as Keyser (b).)
25. Faint traces of wall paintings are visible on the north side of the eastern face of the chancel arch. There appear to be a roundel and a fragment of foliage design.
26. See above p.38-39 and Plate 47B.
27. See above p.23 and Plate 27C.
28. The Moccas tympana will be discussed at length as a separate issue. See below pp.60-63.
29. High Ercall (Shropshire) and Rochford (Worcestershire, but Herefordshire until the 19th century).
30. Morville and Tugford, both Shropshire.
31. Dymock, High Ercall, Kempley, Newnham and Rochford. The Yatton tympanum has been omitted for the moment, although it forms part of this group, but will be dealt with a little latter.
32. Sir A. Clapham in R.C.H.M. (Herefs.), vol.2, p.36.
33. V.C.H. (a), vol.1, p.324.
34. J. Duncumb, vol.2, (Hundred of Broxash) p.79, seems to deny this, stating 'It [Bromyard Church] was anciently stiled a collegiate church, but Bishop Trilleck . . . [14th century] . . . made an entry in his register to this effect: "Ecclasia de Bromyard est ecclesia parochialis, et non ecclesia collegiata, sed porcionaria" '. I have failed to trace this quotation, but on more than one occasion it is termed a parish church. There is, however, a writ, dated 18 June 1352, from the King (Edward III) to Bishop Trilleck (Register 2, p.337, published by Cantilupe Society 1912), which seems to uphold the collegiate status by referring to Bromyard thus: 'in ecclesia collegiata Bromyorde'.
35. V.C.H. (a), vol.1, p.324.
36. Clapham, in R.C.H.M., (Herefs.), vol.2, pp.36-7.
37. *Ibid.,* p.37.
38. Gethyn-Jones, 'An Eleventh Century Tympanum', in W.N.F.C. *Trans.,* vol.37, pt.3,/pp.316-319. (Hereafter cited as Gethyn-Jones (c).) / (1963). See also below pp.73-74.
39. See above pp.37 & below 69.
40. Some of the hollow carving upon the face contains mortar. This suggests that at some time the tympanum was used as simple building material. The most likely period, in view of the Rev. Thomas Rudge's reference to 'Saxon' work at the chancel arch (see Catalogue), would have been the 19th-century rebuilding.
41. The grotesques of the outer order capitals of the chancel at Pauntley have, what appear to be fanned tails.
42. See above pp.36-37.
43. See above p.16.
44. The chevron work on the chancel arch at Bulley is outward-facing, but that on the jamb and arch of the south doorway is not.
45. Sir N. Pevsner, *Northamptonshire* (Buildings of England Series, 1961), p.25. (Hereafter cited as Pevsner (c).)

46. See above, pp.44-48.
47. e.g. in 1870 the north wall of the chancel between the north-east corner of the old central tower and the point where the surviving internal string course begins was destroyed to give access to the new vestries.
48. R.C.H.M. (Herefs.), vol.2, pp.119-20.
49. V.C.H. (a) vol.1, p.312.
50. C. S. Taylor, *An Analysis of the Domesday Survey of Gloucestershire* (1889), pp.100-105.
51. *Ibid.,* p.21.; V.C.H., (a) vol.1, p.283.
52. A. T. Bannister, *The Cathedral Church of Hereford. Its History and Constitution.* (1924), p.132.
53. Bannister, *op.cit.,* p.133.
54. R.C.H.M. (Herefs.), vol.1, p.90.
55. R.C.H.M. *op.cit.,* p.100.
56. J. Round, *Cal. of Doc. Franc.,* 1.409.
57. Clapham (b), p,128.
58. Basically a cushion capital with reed or dart enrichment similar to that upon the Eldersfield capitals.
59. cf. the bases of the blind arcading pillars of the chancel at Bradford-on-Avon.
60. The mask, which is very similar to examples enriching the keystones of the moulding above the beak-headed arches at Elkstone and Siddington (but perhaps a little earlier) should be dated in the third quarter of the 12th century. Perhaps, in view of the generous use of the billet motif at Upleadon's north doorway, this mask may have been the keystone of an arch enriched with much billet work as at Malmesbury.
61. Sir N. Pevsner, *Herefordshire,* (Buildings of England Series, 1963), p.253. (Hereafter cited as Pevsner (a).)
62. R.C.H.M. (Herefs.), vol.1, p.203.
63. R.C.H.M., *op.cit.,* p.204.
64. Zarnecki (a), p.226.
65. Zarnecki (a), p.227.
66. See above p.6 and note for greater detail.
67. See relative sections in R.C.H.M.
68. R.C.H.M. (Herefs.), vol.1. pp.25-6; vol.3, p.134.
69. Zarnecki (b), p.29.
70. See above pp.28-31.
71. Clapham (b), p.137. This is no longer to be seen.

Chapter 8

A Suggested Chronological Table

In this chapter it is proposed to outline a suggested chronological table for the individual examples of sculpture which have been discussed and to place the Dymock group into its proper relationship with certain of the other sculptural groups also found within the medieval diocese of Hereford. It must be stressed that the terms of reference for the study are, of necessity, limited, and in consequence a full overall account of the sculptural development within the determined area (diocesan boundaries) is not implied, nor will it be attempted.

It is clear from the evidence of the composite tympanum at Chepstow Castle, and the presence there of herringbone work and blind arcading,[1] that these distinctive features in wall construction were employed in the West very soon after the Conquest.

In the area under consideration all three of these building methods were in use, and the first two in common use, before the turn of the century. It is not possible, however, to say with certainty that one method found general favour and adoption before the other two; firstly, because examples of each of these constructional characteristics which have survived probably represent only a fraction of the original number; secondly, because there is no documentary evidence by which the local churches containing these early features may be dated. Consequently it is from the churches themselves (and most of them have been much restored, rebuilt or added to in later centuries) that the evidence — such as it is — must come which can suggest a tentative dating sequence.

The use of herringbone work appears to have been restricted to the smaller churches, and not to have been employed locally in the larger ones such as Hereford Cathedral, St. Peters Abbey, Gloucester, now the Cathedral, Leominster Priory and Dymock.[2]

It has been pointed out already that authoritative opinion maintains that herringbone work, as a constructional technique, 'was largely or completely abandoned by the beginning of the 12th century'.[3] This is borne out in Herefordshire and in Gloucestershire, west of the Severn, in two ways:

1. Those churches in West Herefordshire in which there is herringbone work also contain appreciable quantities of tufa, the use of which is recognised as generally indicating an 11th-century date.

2. The churches in which there are composite tympana may be divided into two main groups: those with herringbone work and those without.

The latter are an interesting little group, e.g. Castle Frome[4] and Much Dewchurch. Their doorways and imposts are plain, and their wall courses present a more finished appearance than is the case in the churches containing herringbone work.

It would appear that the herringbone method of wall construction fell out of favour before the use of composite tympanum was discontinued.

The churches containing herringbone work but without composite tympanum vary considerably in their appearance of age, e.g. from Tibberton with its severely plain chancel arch, giving the impression of an early Anglo-Norman date, to Hartpury and Munsley where there is some enrichment of arch, doorway or window splay, and where there is better general 'finish' and standard of workmanship. The same roughness of condition at Tibberton, Mathon and Wigmore — it must be remembered that no original doorways have survived in the first and third churches — is found also at Edvin Loach and Hatfield, and in the wall structure at Bredwardine and Letton — all of which, except Bredwardine, contain both the composite tympanum and herringbone work. It would appear reasonable to conclude that Edvin Loach, Mathon, Tibberton and Wigmore are approximately contemporary,[5] and earlier in date than Hartpury and Munsley.[6] The better appearance and finish of the south doorways at Bredwardine and Letton suggest that — in spite of the general roughness of the wall structures — these two churches ought to be included in the later rather than the earlier of the above groups.

A date c.1080-90 for the earlier group, and one some five to 10 years later for the second group might well be accepted from the evidence of the appearance of the workmanship and the degree of enrichment, bearing in mind the fact that these places appear from their Domesday entries to have been that which they are today, remote country villages without any special importance or significance.

The earlier work at Churcham, i.e. the fragmentary portions of the composite tympanum over the north doorway, the lower stages of the tower with very deep outer splays to the narrow windows and, perhaps, the crude figure now built in above the north doorway, may also be dated to the closing years of the 11th century.

To this same period, as has been pointed out, must be attributed the earlier work at Dymock, Kempley and Preston.[7]

It is reasonable, in view of the composite tympanum with its joggled lintel, and the plainness of the south doorway of the nave and the chancel arch, to assign Much Dewchurch to the early years of the 12th century. Castle Frome, with its two composite and one sunken tympana,[8] and its lack of enrichment and general appearance, and the earlier portions of Hampton Bishop, e.g. south doorway of the nave and the chancel arch, may also be of the same date.

To this same period, approximately, may be attributed the lintels of the Bredwardine group, where the geometrical patterns and lack of real chevron work[9] would suggest a date before c.1115. The Hampton Bishop nave south door lintel also is enriched upon its lower zone with similar geometrical motifs — the upper zone has scale pattern ornamentation, a common enough motif during the early Anglo-Norman period. The lintel, composite tympanum, plain jambs and imposts are out of character with the chevron work — elementary though this example here is — and the mask above the keystone of the arch. Sir Alfred Clapham suggested that the doorway has been reset.[10] This may well be so. A second explanation, however, might be that the doorway was enriched with the chevron arch some years after the doorway had originally been constructed. This, it has been pointed out, happened at Dymock[11] and at Moccas[12] and, possibly, at Pauntley,[13] while lintels were later additions to the doorways at Bredwardine (north and south) and Letton (south).[14] If this explanation is accepted, a date in the first decade of the 12th century, with a possible extension to c.1115, appears reasonable, with the alterations to the south doorway taking place c.1145-60.

The less elaborate form of the tree motif on the reset tympanum at High Ercall, and its asociation with a geometrical border, as against the moulded and pelleted examples of the Dymock and Kempley tympana, would seem to suggest for the High Ercall tympanum an earlier date. On the other hand the similarity of the border motif with that on the Rochford tympanum is most marked, although at the latter place the extreme elaboration of the tree motif and entire enrichment of the doorway weigh against a contemporary date for both the High Ercall and Rochford tympana. On balance, however, it seems reasonable to place the High Ercall tympanum earlier than those of Dymock and Kempley, and a date c.1100-10 would appear to be justified.

The evidence for the second stage of the sculptural development at Dymock and Kempley, and the suggested date for them, have already been fully considered in chapter six, while in chapter seven the date of the examples of the Dymock group of sculpture found in the churches of Bridstow, Bulley, Fownhope, Newnham, Pauntley and Yatton was discussed.

Summary

In summing up the study of the Romanesque sculpture surviving in the Dymock group of churches it would seem reasonable to suggest that there were late 11th-century churches at Dymock, Kempley, and Preston.

At Dymock the survivals of that date appear to be numerous, but scattered, e.g., the blind arcading and the apsidal remains, the string course and pilasters of the north and south walls, the responds and the small tympanum of the central tower block, and the window west of the south doorway.

At Kempley the outline plan (apart from the tower), the stone cross in the vestry, the two small north windows and the smaller east window and the centre stone of the sill of the main east window, and possibly the west doorway, could represent the distinctive remains of the early church.

At Preston the north-west corner of the nave (including the doorway, the two windows and the twin-headed corbel) and the loose piscina capital alone survive of the late 11th-century building.

At a later date — possibly between 1110 and 1120 — Dymock and Kempley underwent alterations. At the former the enrichment of the South doorway was undertaken, while in the latter the south doorway, the chancel arch and the main east window were the places principally affected.

Finally — possibly between 1125 and 1135 — Newnham Church was built (or rebuilt, if the 1016 charter is correct), representing the closing phase of the activities of the Dymock group of sculpture, activities which extend over a period of some 40 years.

It will be seen from the survey of the sculpture of the Dymock group of churches, and from the less detailed study of certain other examples of the Romanesque sculpture surviving in the southern half of the medieval diocese of Hereford, that the early forms of enrichment, cursive, geometrical and classical, which became more elaborate as time passed, began to give way before the grotesque, zoomorphic and other figurative and complicated motifs then coming into more general use.

It will be seen, however, that in spite of the fact that the Dymock group of sculpture, as such, passed, certain of its characteristic motifs continued in use, although the modification in some examples was considerable. This is exemplified by the incorporation of the confronted volutes motif into the work upon the north capital of the outer order of the west doorway (on the inner side) at Leominster (Plate 33B and C), at Rowlstone and at Cusop. Here the design, seen locally in its most primitive state at Dymock, has reached a stage where the parent motif is almost lost in the mature but fanciful work of the mid 12th-century sculptor. The same observation may be made of the tree motif employed on certain tympana of the Dymock group of churches, but in the case of this design the relationship between the later examples at Buildwas and Kilpeck and those of the earlier group of sculpture is more obvious.

NOTES

1. Blind arcading was in use in Anglo-Saxon times, but in a form distinct from that used in the Anglo-Norman period, e.g. on the towers at Earls Barton and Barnack and on the nave and chancel at Bradford-on-Avon. See above, p.5, for details of latest study on the subject of herringbone work.

2. Dymock enjoyed Minster status before the end of the 12th century, see above, p.25.

3. Sir A. Clapham, *Romanesque Architecture in England,* (1950), p.34. (Hereafter cited as Clapham (d).)

4. Pevsner (a), p.99, describes this church as of early Norman date.

5. Tedstone Wafer is in too ruined a condition for any real comment, but from the little that remains, and from the R.C.H.M., vol.2, p.187, description, it seems possible that this church, also may have been contemporary with the earlier group. Rebuildings at Ashleworth and Monkland (there is herringbone work in both churches) makes it impossible to place also these two churches.

6. The absence of tufa at these two churches, and also at Tibberton, has no bearing on the matter, and can be accounted for by the unavailability of that material in this area of the diocese.

7. See above, chapter 6.

8. South doorway of nave, west doorway of nave (Plate 10C) and south doorway of chancel (Plate 56B).

9. The later incised zig-zag pattern across the lintel at Letton and its link-up with the semi-circular moulding of the enclosing arch of the tympanum and its wavy continuation down the jambs (Plate 14A), would suggest a knowledge of the chevron pattern, which Sir Alfred Clapham dates first at Hereford *c.*1110-15, but little experience in its employment.

10. R.C.H.M. (Herefs.), vol.2, p.86.

11. See above pp.27-31.

12. See above pp.60-63.

13. See above pp. 49-52.

14. See above pp.10 and 11-12.

Suggested Chronological Table

Date Bracket	Building	Main Features
c.1070	Chepstow Castle	Blind Arcading, Composite Tympanum, Herringbone work, Pilasters.
	Church	
c.1080-90	Edvin Loach	Composite Tympanum, Herringbone work, Tufa.
	Hatfield	Composite Tympanum, Herringbone work, Step feature, Tufa.
	Mathon	Heavy Lintels, Herringbone work.
	Moccas	Entirely built of Tufa, except for dressings (arches and doorways).
	Tibberton	Herringbone work.
	Wigmore	Herringbone work.
c.1090-1100	Ashleworth	Herringbone work.
	Bredwardine	Herringbone work, Tufa.
	Bromyard	Font, Peter & Cross Stones over the South doorway of the Nave.
	Churcham	Composite tympanum (part), Figured stone, Tower (Lower stages).
	Dymock	Blind Arcading, Capitals (Central tower), Pilasters, Plain Tympanum, String course).
	Hartpury	Herringbone work.
	Kempley	Loft East Window, Ridge Cross (in Vestry), West doorway, North Windows.
	Letton	Composite Tympanum, Herringbone work, String Course, Tufa.
	Linton	String Course.
	Munsley	Herringbone work.
	Preston (nr. Dymock)	North doorway (with Tympanum), Piscina Capital (loose), Twin headed Corbel.
c.1100-1115	Bredwardine	Lintels (North & South Doorways), Capitals of the South Doorways.
	Castle Frome	Composite and Recessed Tympana (South and West Doorways).
	Hampton Bishop	Chancel Arch, South Doorway (part), Tower?
	High Ercall	Tympanum (re-used).
	Letton	Lintel (South doorway).
	Much Dewchurch	Chancel Arch, South Doorway (with Step feature), Cross Fragments.
	Willersley	Lintel.
c.1110-1125	Dymock	Alterations to South Doorway (Tympanum and Arch added).
	Kempley	Alterations to (1) East Window, (2), Chancel Arch, (3) South Doorway.
c.1125-1145	Bridstow	Chancel arch.
	Bulley	Chancel arch.
	Churcham	Capital (broken and built into South wall of the Nave).
	Fownhope	Central Tower.
	Moccas	Enrichment on Arch and Doorways.
	Newnham	Capitals and Tympanum - all loose, Font, Recess over North doorway.
	Pauntley	Alterations to the Chancel Arch and South Doorway of the Nave.
	Rochford	Chancel Arch and North doorway of the Nave (including tympanum).
	Yatton (nr. Kempley)	South doorway of the Nave (including Tympanum).
1140-1160	Buildwas	Tympanum.
	Upleadon	Mask over the Chancel Arch, North Doorway of the Nave.

All reference to examples of the Herefordshire School of Sculpture to be found in the churches listed above, e.g. Tympanum at Fownhope, has been deliberately omitted.

Chapter 9

Probable Sources of the
Dymock Group of Sculpture

An attempt will now be made to identify the sources which may have inspired the paired and the stepped ram's-headed volutes and the tree motif of the tympana which distinguish and constitute the Dymock group of sculpture.

The Large Stepped Volute

The earliest Anglo-Norman volutes in this country which can, at present, be closely dated are those in the chapel of Durham Castle (c.1070), Canterbury Cathedral crypt (c.1075), St. John's Chapel in the Tower of London (c.1080), and Gloucester Cathedral crypt (c.1084). All these are bulbous in form and are in marked contrast with the flat incised examples at the south doorways of Dymock and Pauntley Churches, and even with the convex specimens surviving in the other churches, e.g., Bridstow, Kempley and Newnham. There are, it is true, in the derelict church of Theon (a few miles north-west of Caen), where the tower is of 11th-century date, flattish volutes which, in some measure, can compare with the incised ones of the Dymock group, but even in these the similarity is not pronounced. The examples of the local group have, in addition, the distinctive stepped feature.

The earliest of the surviving large volute capitals of the Dymock type is the loose pillar piscina head from Preston Church,[1] enriched with leaf and ram's-head motifs — the latter with protruding stepped tongue (Plate 27C). The later examples of this type of capital,[2] as has been stated,[3] lost their zoomorphic reality and became fully stylised, retaining, however, clear relationships with the Preston prototype. This last, if forming part of the original church, must be of late 11th-century date.

The only other local capitals with a ram's-head carved at the corners are in Hereford Cathedral. The first is a 19th-century replacement capital in the presbytery North arcade; the second, its predecessor maybe, is amongst those deposited in the Vicars' cloister.[4] The latter is a capital on which is carved at two corners a crude ram's-head, with horns forming a rough volute on each side (Plate 26A). The volute is flat, but in this respect alone can a comparison be made between it and the capitals of the Dymock group.

Capitals having rams'-heads with the horns forming the volute were not unusual in the Byzantine world from the 6th century onwards. There are (amongst others) examples in the Archaeological Museum at Istanbul and in the Archiepiscopal and National Museums (Plate 27A) in Ravenna. Similar rams'-headed and voluted capitals are present in La Trinité Cathedral in Caen (Plate 25 C & D) and dated c.1070. A ram's head with an elongated five-leafed sprig protruding from the mouth (Plate 27B), calling to mind the stepped tongue at Preston, taking the place of a spur upon the plinth of a pier, is found in Worms Cathedral. This late Carolingian cathedral (unlike that of Cologne) underwent extensive rebuilding soon after the middle of the 12th century. It must be assumed, therefore, that the plinth with its ram's-head must date after 1150, but it is quite conceivable that in this carving the sculptor was following an earlier example.

Robert of Lorraine became Bishop of Hereford in 1079, and during his episcopate built the Bishop's chapel which was partly demolished in 1737. This two-tiered chapel, sketches of which made by Stukeley before its demolition and now lodged in the library of the Society of Antiquaries, is a design found in Burgundy and Lorraine.

This building was unique in Britain. Consequently it is reasonable to assume that workmen, or at least a master-mason, would have been brought over from the Rhineland to undertake or supervise the construction.[5]

Sir Alfred Clapham stated that the only documentary evidence of the date of the beginning of the existing cathedral is a statement in the Calendar of Obits[6] that Bishop Reinhelm (1107-15) was its founder. Sir Alfred then expressed the opinion that the east end, presbytery, east towers and south transept and the treasury to the east were probably begun early in the 12th century. Most authorities have followed a similar line for dating the cathedral. This would place the ejected capitals[7] within the first or second decade of the 12th-century.

A small tympanum built into the north wall of the north triforium at Hereford Cathedral was mentioned both by Sir Alfred Clapham and by Mr. G. Marshall, but neither attributed to it any special significance. In June 1963 this was removed from its position and was examined by

Professor Zarnecki and myself (Plate 18A-C).[8] The tympanum (overall measurement 1ft 6½in. by 11½in.), which had been *in situ,* had been over a filled-in narrow window of approximately 8in. by 30in. — figures almost identical with the original north windows in Kempley Church. A primitive tree motif was carved upon the stone. Professor Zarnecki pointed out that the treatment of the leaves was similar to that employed in certain of the capitals at Payerne Priory in Switzerland which are dated *c.*1070. Window tympana are uncommon. The ones at Stoke-sub-Hamdon (Somerset) (Plate 44B) and Tangmere (Sussex) (Plate 44A) are of late 11th-century date.[9] Those over the two windows in the North wall of the chancel in Tarrington, Herefordshire, (Plate 44C) may also be of the same period. Professor Zarnecki, in his F.C. Morgan Memorial lecture at Hereford on 17 December 1963, confirmed the late 11th-century date for the small window tympanum lately removed, and stated that this would indicate a date for the east end of the cathedral some 20 to 30 years earlier than was previously accepted. This strengthens the belief that Bishop Robert of Lorraine was the designer and originator of the Anglo-Norman cathedral, although he may not have lived to see the completion even of the presbytery and transepts. The massive piers in the presbytery and the east aisle terminal towers would not be out of keeping with this earlier date. The latter feature, not found in Normandy but favoured in West Germany,[10] added to the fact of the design of the demolished Bishop's Chapel is additional corroboration of the impress of Robert of Lorraine and of Lotharingian influence. It is thus reasonable to accept the possibility of similar Lotharingian and Rhenish influence behind the large stylised voluted capitals of the Dymock group.

There are, in the chancel of St. Mary's, Kempley, remarkable wall paintings dating from the 12th century.[11] The subject, common throughout Christendom of that period, is the Majesty. The format — Christ flanked by the 12 apostles seated within niches — is one which has no surviving parallel in this country. On the Continent a somewhat similar composition is found on the chancel vault of Notre Dame la Grande in Poitiers and in the crypt of St. Savin. The closest parallels, however, would appear to be in such churches as St. Georges, Oberzell (Lake Constance) and in certain German manuscripts, e.g. Codex Egberti (fol. 102v) and the Gospel Lectionary of Heinrich II, fol. 202r.

In spite of this basic influence the whole execution of the volute, with its emphasis more upon incised work than upon undercarving, displays some affinity with the low relief on Saxon crosses and other monuments. The stepped tongue patterns, furthermore, could be a stylisation of the foliage motif found, as mentioned, at Worms Cathedral and also in

Ravenna at the entrance to the so-called Palace of Theodoric (attributed to the 9th or 10th century) where the square capitals have in relief single volutes, from the junction of which are pendant trifoliated sprigs (Plate 27A), suggestive of truncated examples of the Worms Cathedral specimen and (in a modified form) of the stepped pattern of the Dymock group. It has been pointed out already that the stepped pattern, a feature of Anglo-Saxon decoration and design from the 7th century, was widely employed between the Cotswolds and the Black Mountains both in the late Anglo-Saxon and early Anglo-Norman periods. It must be mentioned, too, that a continuous stepped pattern is painted upon the east face of the outer order of the chancel arch at Kempley, and that this painted pattern is found both in German manuscripts (e.g. Codex Gertrudianus)[12] and in Italian mosaics as well as in Anglo-Saxon work of all kinds, e.g. the Lindisfarne Gospels.

CODEX GERTRUDIANUS

(by courtesy of Professor G. Zarnecki and the Courtauld Institute of Art).

It can be said, to epitomize, that the inspirations behind these large stepped volutes appear to be conflicting. It is, however, reasonable to suggest, in view of the lead back from the pillar piscina at Preston, through the probable late 11th century ram's-headed capital in Hereford to the Empire and back to early Christian monuments in such centres as Ravenna, and because of the prevalence of Anglo-Saxon design and native labour, that the immediate influence was imported, but that there occurred a major modification through local interpretation.

Small Paired Volutes

Confronted volutes as capital enrichment is a motif which, apart from the examples named,[13] has not survived — if ever it existed — in this area. It is a design which has been used in some countries in general ornament-ation, however, from early times, e.g. St. George's, Salonica, 5th century enrichment in the dome. It is a design employed more frequently in its alternative form, i.e. a confronted pair of small volutes at the centre of an arch, or lintel, or other bands to be decorated, with the remaining volutes following, in series, away from the centre, the inclination of its companion. The absence in this district of further examples of the confronted motif surviving from the Anglo-Norman period is surprising, for with the six examples displaying four different stages of development of the design, spread over some 30 to 40 years, it might have been expected that some companions to the Dymock, Kempley or Newnham works of sculpture would have survived, suggesting perhaps a source of inspiration stretching back to some continental centre.

It may be of interest to record that a gold ring, thought to be Saxon or Irish and dated *c.* 10th century,[14] was found in Berkeley Castle before 1800.[15] The central raised boss (diam. 15mm) is enriched with a hoop. Inside the circle, and dividing the surface area into quarters, are four pairs of confronted volutes. These are similar in design to the pairs in Dymock Church.

There are locally, however, examples of a pre-Conquest motif which may well have had some influence upon the evolution of the confronted volute design. The continuous spiral is a primitive design which has been almost universally employed. Its use in Britain during the Anglo-Saxon period was widespread both in manuscript illumination and for sculptural enrichment. One of the variants of this basic motif enriches the main central band of the font bowl at Deerhurst[16] (Plate 57A) which is 12 miles distant from Dymock. A similar design is carved upon a fragment of a stone cross base at Elmstone-Hardwick. This church is only four miles from Deerhurst, and it may be assumed, in view of the close resemblance between the carving upon the font and cross and cross base, that these two monuments are contemporary, and the product of a common workshop. The complete lack of evidence indicating a positive line of approach leading to a probable source of inspiration behind the distinctive series of confronted volutes of the Dymock group of sculpture suggests the possibility that the carving of the earliest example of these confronted volutes (Dymock) was executed by a mason following pre-Conquest work such as the Deerhurst or Elmstone-Hardwick motif.

Tympana Motif

The tree design carved upon the tympana of the Dymock group of sculpture is a variation of a motif common to many countries in Europe and the Middle East from earliest days. Variants of this basic motif were used so frequently and widely in church architecture of Western Europe of the 11th and 12th centuries that it would seem impossible at first sight to point with certainty to a probable line of descent from any particular source of inspiration or influence.

The tree motif of the Dymock group of sculpture has, however, one feature which distinguishes it from all other examples of tree or foliage enrichments upon tympana or capitals in Britain or indeed in Western Europe of which I have knowledge. It is this peculiarity which, although it cannot point to any parallel amongst the sculpture in this country or on the Continent, can by its very localisation suggest a possible answer to the problem of inspiration. It will be noticed that the tree motif enriching the tympana of the Dymock group[17] has a large bare branch shooting out from either side of the main stem.[18] The six examples of the foliage motif carved upon tympana and the one known example of enriching another feature, i.e. a font in Bromyard Church, display considerable variation in the interpretation of the basic idea. It is noticeable, nevertheless, that however much the leaf design varied the distinguishing characteristic, i.e. the bare branch with cross or bud-head, maintained its prominence.

The most ornate and perhaps, bearing in mind the greater variety of enrichment and design of the whole doorway, the latest of this group of tympana is at Rochford (Plate 20C). The High Ercall example, unfortunately only a relic built into a new body, is the plainest, and probably the earliest upon a tympanum.

There is a cruder form of this motif carved upon the font in Bromyard Church. Crudity cannot be taken always to indicate an earlier date; but when the finer workmanship is found in the less important buildings, and when the more primitive form is upon a piece of furniture, as against the main structure, the inference must be that the cruder form represents an earlier date. Consequently, remembering the status of Bromyard and High Ercall Churches[19] as indicated by the Domesday Survey, it may be assumed that the Bromyard font is earlier in date than the High Ercall tympanum.

The 'Dymock' tree motif occupies but a third of the area of the upper zone on the Bromyard font bowl. The remaining two thirds are enriched with what Professor Pevsner describes as a 'running scroll motif'.[20] This running foliage design may perhaps supply the evidence needed to suggest with some confidence one of the sources from which the peculiar tree motif of the Dymock group of sculpture was derived. Running scroll is not a motif of Norman inspiration, but rather a harking back to Anglo-Saxon convention, and based upon pre-Conquest manuscript and stone-carving designs. The inspiration behind the scroll work upon the Bromyard font would appear to be Anglo-Saxon rather than Norman, and yet the symmetrical form of the 'Dymock' design upon the font is more suggestive of a Cluniac or Bernay influence. Looking again at the tympanum of Rochford, it is noticeable that though the motif (Plate 20C) follows the lines of the conventional foliage capital designs the symmetry is broken, and young shoots emerge from the lateral branches in a manner more akin to Anglo-Saxon treatment. It will be observed (Plate 19B and C) that the Dymock and Kempley tympana designs lack balance, that (a) the middle sections of each side do not match in the way expected of a Norman figure, and (b) the designs at Dymock and Kempley are reversed, i.e. left for right and right for left. It would seem, therefore, that there has been some Anglo-Saxon influence behind at least the motif at Bromyard and at Rochford, which probably are the earliest and latest examples of the tree or foliage motif found in the Dymock group.

The bare branch with cross or buds termination may supply evidence of another influence behind the formation of this characteristic tympanum motif. The motif is usually referred to as the Tree of Life, and to it a symbolic meaning has often been attributed.[21] The cross, early in the Christian era, became identified with man's salvation,[22] and , soon, with Christ Himself as the divine source of life. The bare branches with the cross or bud feature may be an attempt to remind those entering the church that from the tree came the cross through which flowed man's salvation, or else (if the terminals are intended as buds and not crosses) that from the dead branch (or death on the tree of Calvary) sprang new-born life, i.e. the perpetual miracle of Spring pointing to the Resurrection and Eternal Life through Christ.

There is in the British Museum a manuscript, believed to have been connected with the Imperial Schools at Aachen and c.800,[23] which has on fol.6v an illumination (Plate 22B) in which a palm tree is represented with leaves. The head of the tree is crowned with a cross on which the terminals are built up on the step pattern. Halfway up the trunk, and issuing from the leaf group, is (on both sides) a long stemmed flower. The whole effect of the leaves and flowers (although more ornate, elaborate and finished) is suggestive of the tympanum motif of the Dymock group of sculpture. Once again in the case of the tympanum the lead appears to go back to the Franco-German border, and to the centre of the Empire, which, remembering the Lotharingian origins of the Hereford Bishops of 1061-95, is, perhaps, understandable. Thus the characteristic features of the Dymock group of monuments appear, in general, to be the result of a combination of foreign and native influences.

NOTES
1. Now in Gloucester Museum.
2. e.g. Bridstow, Bulley, Kempley and Pauntley (chancel arch).
3. See above p.31.
4. See above pp.13-14 and R.C.H.M. (Herefs.), vol. 1.p. 114.
5. See Professor J. Bony for the latest study of this building. 'La chapelle épiscopale de Hereford et les apports Lorraine en Angleterre après la conqûete', in *Actes du XIXe Congres International d'Histoire de l'Art,* (Paris 1959), pp.36-43. On p.40 he states, 'Etant l'oeuvre d'un architecte tres certainement venu de Lorraine'.
6. R.C.H.M. (Herefs.), vol.1, p.90.
7. See above pp.13-14.
8. W.N.F.C. *Trans,* vol.37, pt.3, pp.316-19, (1963) for general description and an account of its removal.
9. Sir N. Pevsner, *South and West Somerset,* (Buildings of England Series, 1958), p.304 for Stoke-sub-Hamdon. (Hereafter cited as Pevsner (b).)
10. e.g. St. Kastor, Coblenz; see Clapham (d), p.32.
11. Gethyn-Jones (b).
12. Codex Gertrudianus, f.9, at Cividale, Museo Archeologico Nazionale.
13. Dymock (earliest), Kempley, Newnham, Cusop, Leominster and Rowlstone.
14. H. Clifford-Smith, *Jewellery,* (The Connoisseur's Library, 1908), p.37, Plate XIII[10]. The small confronted volute motif in series within a circle — similar in pattern to the motif upon the Berkeley ring — is also found upon a 9th-century cross at Irton, Lancs. Sir A. Clapham, *English Romanesque Architecture before the Conquest,* (1930), Plate 17. (Hereafter cited as Clapham (a).)
15. B. and G. Arch. Soc. *Trans.,* vol.48, (1926), Plate 1 opposite p.176.
16. The two zones — above and below the main band of decoration — of scroll or vine character will be considered when dealing with the tympanum design.
17. Dymock, High Ercall, Kempley, Newnham, Rochford and Yatton. The tympana at Morville and Tugford are too weathered for the motif to be seen clearly.
18. The branch has a cross formation or triple bud feature at its extremity (Plates 19-21).
19. See above pp.53-54.
20. Pevsner (a), p.92.
21. See above p.16-17.
22. *Archaeologia,* vol.81 (1931), pp.49-61.
23. B. M. Harley MS., 2788. A similar illumination is found on fol.7r of the same MS. Here the long stemmed flower is present, as is the bud formation. The step pattern feature, however, is absent.

Chapter 10

Conclusions

(a) The Sculpture

In the preceding chapters an attempt has been made to establish the fact that within the southern half of the medieval diocese of Hereford there is a group of sculpture which is distinctive in character and of which the surviving examples are numerous — more numerous, indeed, than was first believed. It was sought, also, to establish its date and its place in the development of local sculpture. It has been pointed out that there are 13 churches[1] within this group and that they contain 30 examples of one or other of the three motifs.

In conclusion, it will be seen that the group of monuments discussed in this study presents a fairly homogeneous style which lasted, with modifications, over a period of some 30 years or 40 years. Clearly, the number of buildings involved is such that it must be assumed that a number of craftsmen were involved in their erection and decoration. This is also implied by the stylistic and technical variations between the monuments. Thus, on the one hand, the monuments here discussed form a group linked by stylistic, iconographic and technical similarities; on the other hand, the monuments are found in close proximity, occupying the southern half of the medieval diocese of Hereford, and they all date within a comparatively short period. These conditions are sufficient to justify the assumption that more than one workshop was involved and that, therefore, it can be claimed that the Dymock Group is in fact the Dymock School of Sculpture. For it will be remembered that the school of Romanesque sculpture as defined by that great French scholar Professor Louis Bréhier[2] has to fulfil the following conditions before it deserves the title of a school. The sculpture of a certain type must be common to the whole production of a region and it must develop over a certain period of time. This sculpture must be peculiar to that region, and to that region alone, and it can be identified by its method of application to architecture, by its technique, by its style and by its iconography. The sculpture which is the subject of this study fulfils all these conditions and it may therefore be considered a School.

(b) The Sources

It would appear that there are three factors which need to be remembered when considering the evolution of the characteristic motifs of the sculpture of the Dymock School.

Firstly, there must have existed the obvious and powerful driving force of Normandy, demonstrated broadly by the rebuilding in this country of all cathedrals and many abbeys and parish churches during the century following the Conquest. This was effected through the agencies of the new ecclesiastical hierarchy[3] and of the great Norman landowners.[4] The distinctive character of the local sculpture, however, with the small volutes, the flat and stylised form of the volute with its stepped tongue, and the irregularities of the tree motif, especially the running scroll work on the Bromyard font and the shoots upon the Rochford tympanum, and the bare branches with cross or bud terminals present on all seven examples of this design, distinguishes the monuments of the Dymock School from the other comparable Anglo-Norman works of sculpture.

Secondly, it seems probable that local, native influences were at work, that Anglo-Saxon techniques, style and patterns survived the Conquest and made themselves felt in buildings, paintings and sculpture long after the transfer of both civil and ecclesiastical power to foreign hands.

Throughout much of Britain native customs and culture tended to wither and die under the over-riding influences of the Norman conquerors. In the West this process was not as rapid, nor as final, as in many other parts of the country. Might this have been due to the fact that 20 years after the Conquest the See of Worcester alone retained its pre-Conquest Bishop? Is it possible that Saxon Wulstan commanded such respect with the new masters that this feeling was reflected in a greater spirit of consideration for native susceptibilities and achievement, and a fuller appreciation of local conditions than was evident elsewhere? It was due, maybe, to the fact that Norman penetration and domination were less complete, that geographical realities and ethnological factors combined to produce conditions in which physical resistance and cultural persistence were made possible. It is conceivable that some such factors operated in the medieval diocese of Hereford which could account for the persistence of pre-Conquest sculptural techniques and decorative designs. Most probably, however, it can be accounted for by the law of supply and demand, that the volume of buildings was so great that it was both natural and necessary to employ local talent to complete the heavy programme of church building undertaken during the century following the Norman conquest of Britain.

The third factor to be considered is the extent of influence from Lorraine and the Rhineland during the 11th and 12th centuries upon architecture, sculpture and painting in the West of England, where a number of Lorrainer bishops had been appointed. The diocese of Hereford was not unaffected by these trends.

Sir Alfred Clapham, towards the end of his life[5] and writing in the light of vast personal experience, substantially supported the fact of Lotharingian and Rhenish influence upon English arts and architecture during this period. He made it clear, while maintaining that 'the post-Conquest architecture of England was predominantly an offshoot of the Norman School of Romanesque', that to him it was 'becoming more and more apparent that this fact can only be accepted with very definite qualifications. The foreign influences which so strongly affected the Court and policy of King Edward the Confessor (1042-66) were not entirely Norman'.[6] Sir Alfred quoted the following passage from William of Poitiers, chaplain to William the Conqueror, in support of this fact: 'the women of England are as skilful with the needle and gold embroidery as their menfolk excell in every craft. *Moreover Germans most knowing in such arts were wont to settle among them*'.[7]

Architecture

The Bishop's Chapel at Hereford, built by Bishop Robert of Lorraine (1079-95), and largely destroyed in 1737,[8] is an obvious example of such influence.

Professor Jean Bony in his short study of this building (La chapelle épiscopale de Hereford et les apports Lorrains en Angleterre après la conquête) expressed the opinion that 'the chapel of Hereford is not only a system of considerable retrospective significance for the historian, for in England the arrival of this travelling master from Lorraine had immediate and important consequences, but it might even be that this rediscovered [newly recognised?] chapel constitutes [gives us?] the key to all the styles of the West of England'.[9]

It is now clear that Hereford Cathedral, too, was probably begun during Robert's episcopate.[10] There is ample evidence for the existence of the destroyed towers flanking the east end of the choir aisles. They have been compared by Sir Alfred Clapham with those at St. Kastor, Coblenz,[11] and must be considered as resulting from Rhineland influence. Sir Alfred also pointed out that at Hereford Cathedral 'the arch opening into the former main apse [3 apse type] is comparatively low and not at all in the Norman manner'.[12]

The same authority described the arrangement of the transeptal towers of Old Sarum Cathedral — begun by Bishop Harmann of Lorraine — and of Exeter Cathedral as probably deriving 'from the Rhineland, where it can be seen at Murbach in Alsace'.[13]

The pyramidal capping of Sompting Church tower (helm-form) follows a pattern, Sir Alfred points out, 'common in western Germany'.[14] The post-Conquest church at Churcham[15] has a tower similarly roofed. This might be a further instance of the extent of Rhineland influence within the Hereford diocese and Dymock group of churches.

It is as conceivable that the high percentage of apsidal parish churches within the medieval diocese of Hereford, when compared with the neighbouring counties of Gloucester, Shropshire, Monmouth and Worcester (Ch.6, pp.24-25), resulted as much from German as from Norman influence.

Sculpture

Lotharingian and Rhenish influences upon stone sculpture within the medieval diocese of Hereford have already been referred to in the main text, e.g.

(a) The figures carved upon the Letton lintel which are so markedly similar to illuminations in Chronicon Zwifaltense Minus f.6v.[16]

(b) The tympanum motif distinctive of the Dymock School which may well be based upon an Aachen manuscript.[17]

(c) The ram's head (whether zoomorphic or stylised) with stepped tongue which forms the volute so frequently found in the Dymock School looks back via the Empire to Early Christian sculpture of Ravenna, Rome and Constantinople.[18]

In lead sculpture, too, the same influences may be detected.

Professor Zarnecki in his monograph *English Romanesque Lead Sculpture*[19] pointed out that it was probably from Lower Lorraine that both France and England took the idea of making fonts in metal (p.3). He also stressed the importance of the Bury Bible upon manuscript decoration, wall-painting and even stone sculpture (p.6), adding that this manuscript 'seems to have affinities with the art of the Duchy of Lower Lorraine'. On page 11 the professor draws attention to the Hereford Troper,[20] which has been accepted generally as 'influenced by Mosan art'. (p.12). It is considered that the unique set of six 12th-century lead fonts in Gloucestershire — one of which, Oxenhall, is in a parish which marches with Dymock and Kempley, and three of which, Oxenhall, Tidenham and Lancaut, came from the same medieval rural deanery — reveal dependence upon Mosan sources. The professor's conclusions (page 23) go even farther: 'One cannot over-emphasize the importance of the influence on English lead fonts, that came from Lower Lorraine. . .If, in the south east of England, the influence from Lorraine at about 1150 was something new, in the west part of the country connections with Lorraine date back to pre-Conquest times'.

Paintings

The Kempley frescoes must be considered. Most authorities, including Tristram, Wormald and Weaver, have looked to Spain and Western France for the artistic sources behind these paintings. It is true that the latter have much in common in subject matter with wall-paintings at Tavent, Poitiers, St. Savin and Montoire. Yet, as has been pointed out,[21] the differences are considerable, while the similarities between the Kempley works and manuscript illuminations such as are found in the Codex Egberti (fol.102v) and wall paintings at, for example, St. Georges, Oberzell, are so apparent that a relationship with the latter may be assumed.

Westlake, almost alone among the 19th and 20th century authorities, argues that the Kempley paintings, while showing resemblances to Spanish and French wall-paintings display closer affinities with German examples.[22]

It may well be that:

(a) the artists employed at Oberzell and Kempley worked from a common model

or

(b) the Kempley artist had before him a pattern book based upon the porch paintings at Oberzell or others of the same school, now lost

or

(c) a German artist brought over by Bishop Robert to decorate his chapel stayed on and was later employed at Kempley, or that an English pupil taught by him worked at Kempley.

It is clear from the foregoing statements of Professor Zarnecki, Professor Bony, Sir Alfred Clapham and Mr. Westlake that they substantially support the thesis that Lotharingian and Rhenish influence can be traced in many aspects of art development in the West of England, and especially within the medieval diocese of Hereford, during the 11th and early 12th century.

Final Assessment

Thus it seems reasonable, in the light of available evidence, to assume that the essential features which distinguish the monuments of the Dymock School from the customary Anglo-Norman sculpture were imparted by Anglo-Saxon and Rhenish treatment and interpretation which modified the Norman design and produced a hybrid peculiar to the southern half of the medieval diocese of Hereford.

NOTES

1. Ten of these churches are within a 12-mile radius of Dymock.
2. L. Bréhier, 'Les traits originaux de iconographie dans la sculpture romane de l'Auvergne', in *Medieval Studies,* vol,2, (1939), pp.389 ff.
3. Including Norman foundations, e.g. Cormeilles, which owned such local churches as Dymock, Linton, Newent and Pauntley.
4. e.g. the de Laci family.
5. He died in 1951.
6. Clapham (d), p.24.
7. *Ibid.,* p.23.
8. W.N.F.C. *Trans.,* 1957, pp.256-60.
9. 'Mais la chapelle de Hereford n'est pas seulement un symptôme riche de signification rétrospective pour l'historien: en Angleterre l'arrivée de ce maître lorrain voyageur a eu des conséquences immediates et importantes. Il se pourait même que cette chapelle retrouvée nous donne la clef de tout le style de l'Ouest de l'Angleterre'. J. Bony, *op.cit.,* p.42.
10. W.N.F.C. *Trans.,* 1963, p.316-19; see also above, pp.73-74.
11. Clapham (d), p.32; R.C.H.M. (Herefs.), vol.1, p.92, 'a feature unparalleled in this country'.
12. Clapham (d), p.32.
13. *Ibid.,*
14. *Ibid.,* p.21
15. See above pp. 48-49.
16. Chronicon Zwifaltense Minus f.6v, Stuttgart; see above p.6, and also W.N.F.C., *Trans.,* 1966, pp.136-9.
17. B. M. Harley MS., 2788, fol,6v and 7.
18. See above, p.74-76.
19. G. Zarnecki, *English Romanesque Lead Sculpture* (1957).
20. B.M. MS. Caligula A.14., c.1040.
21. See above, p.74.
22. e.g. Oberzell, Fulda and Goldbach.

Catalogue

A detailed catalogue of the 16 churches containing the principal motifs of the Dymock School of Sculpture was included at this point in the original thesis.

The publication of the Gloucestershire, Herefordshire, Shropshire and Worcestershire volumes of the Penguin Buildings of England Series renders the catalogue unnecessary. It must, however, be emphasized that this does not imply full agreement with all the statements, interpretations or suggestions made in those works.

Bibliography

In the interests of economy the bibliographical section of the thesis has been omitted.

An extensive bibliography covering the 11th to 13th centuries will be found in:

1. Lawrence Stone   Sculpture in Britain: The Middle Ages,
   The Pelican History of Art Series, 1955.

2. Geoffrey Webb   Architecture in Britain, The Middle Ages,
   The Pelican History of Art Series, 1956.

The general reader will find the following books of considerable interest:

1. Baldwin Brown   The Arts in Early England, vol.ii,
   (Anglo-Saxon Architecture) 2nd Ed., London, 1925.

2. A. W. Clapham   (a) English Romanesque Architecture before the Conquest, Oxford, 1930.
   (b) English Romanesque Architecture after the Conquest, Oxford 1934.

3. C. E. Keyser   Norman Tympana and Lintels in the churches of Great Britain, 2nd Ed., London, 1927.

4. Royal Commission on Historical Monuments, Herefordshire, vols. i-iii, London, 1931-34.

5. L. Stone   As above.

6. G. Webb   As above.

7. G. Zarnecki   (a) English Romanesque Sculpture 1066-1140, London, 1951.
   (b) English Romanesque Sculpture 1140-1210, London, 1953.
   (c) English Romanesque Lead Sculpture, London, 1957.

Index of Persons

Index of Places

Index of Sculpture

The Plates

Pre-Conquest Survivals

1. a. St. Giles Church, Acton Beauchamp, Herefordshire. Anglo-Saxon Cross-Shaft re-used as a Lintel over the south doorway of the west tower.

b. St. James Church, Cradley, Herefordshire. Anglo-Saxon frieze re-used in north wall of the west tower.

c. St. Andrew's Church, Churcham, Gloucestershire. Tablet (16ins. x 13ins.) built into the wall above the north doorway of the nave. Anglo-Saxon? 11th-century post-Conquest?

2. a. St. Mary's Priory Church,
Deerhurst, Gloucestershire.
Triangular surround to the Deerhurst
Angel. South wall. The only surviving
bay of the polygonal apse.

b. St. James Church, Tedstone-Delamere, Herefordshire.
Triangular strip-label in tufa, north doorway of the nave.

3. St. Mary's Church, Newent, Gloucestershire. a. and b. Situated in a case at the west end of the nave c. and d. Cross-shaft in the porch.

4. a. South doorway of the nave, St. Peter's Church, Bromyard, Herefordshire. 1. St. Peter; 2. Cross.

b. St. Peter's Church, Stanton Lacy, Salop. North wall of the nave. 1. Cross above doorway; 2. above this a bracket with four pellets.

Chepstow Castle—The Great Keep

5. a. Tympanum over east doorway of lowest stage of the Keep. Note stones set diagonally

b. Blind arcading in west wall (second stage) of the Keep. Note diagonal pattern at the head of the second bay from the south. The pattern is formed in the plaster

c. Chapel in Caen Castle. Doorway at west end. Tympanum pattern is similar to that at Chepstow. This is a photograph of a plate in J. S. Cotman's *Architectural Antiquities of Normandy* (1822).

Plate 48

6. Gloucester Cathedral Crypt

Herringbone Work

7. (a) St. James Church, Wigmore, Herefordshire.

b. St. Leonard's Church, Hatfield,
Herefordshire. North wall of the nave

c. The Holy Trinity Church, Tibberton,
Gloucestershire. West end of the north wall of the
chancel

8. a. Ruined Church of Perriers, Normandy. West wall of the nave. This is a photograph of a plate in J. S. Cotman's *Architectural Antiquities of Normandy* (1822). Plate 68

b. St. Bartholomew's Church, Munsley, Herefordshire. East wall of chancel

Composite Tympana

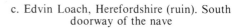

9. a. (above left) St. Leonard's Church, Hatfield, Herefordshire. North doorway of the nave. Note the Joggled Lintel

b. (*above right*) St. David's Church, Much Dewchurch, Herefordshire. South doorway of the nave. Note the Joggled Lintel

c. Edvin Loach, Herefordshire (ruin). South doorway of the nave

d. St. Andrew's Church, Churcham, Gloucestershire. North doorway of the nave

10. a. St. John Baptist Church, Letton, Herefordshire. South doorway of the nave

b. Letton. West doorway of the nave

c. St. Michael's Church, Castle Frome, Herefordshire. West end of the nave. Note also shallow pilaster

11. a. St. Michael's Church, Michaelchurch, Herefordshire. North doorway of the nave (blocked). Later window

b. St. Giles Church, Aston, Herefordshire. South doorway of the nave, now leading from the vestry

c. St. Andrew's Church, Hampton Bishop, Herefordshire. South doorway of the nave

12. a. (*above left*) St. John Baptist Church, Mathon, Herefordshire. South doorway of the nave

b. (*above right*) Mathon, north doorway of the nave

c. La Trinité, Caen, Normandy. Entrance to tower stairway, south-west corner of the nave

d. The Holy Trinity Church, Tibberton, Gloucestershire. Chancel arch

Lintels of the Bredwardine Group (Herefordshire)

13. a. St. Andrew's Church, Bredwardine. North doorway (blocked)

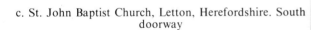

b. Bredwardine. South doorway

c. St. John Baptist Church, Letton, Herefordshire. South doorway

d. St. Mary Magdalene Church, Willersley. South doorway

14. a. Cushion capital carved on roll moulding
b. *(below left)* (a) heads; (b) animals
c. (*below right*) St. Croix Church, St. Lo, Normandy.
Photograph taken of a plate in J. S. Cotman's *Architectura*
Antiquities of Normandy (1822). Plate 88

Signs of the Zodiac and the Labours of the Months

15. All photographs of plates in *Gislebertus: Sculptor of Autun* by Abbe D. Grivot and Professor G. Zarnecki

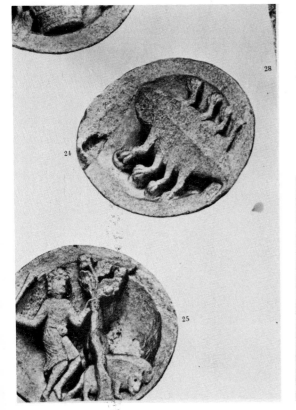

a. *(above left) Chronicon Zwifaltense Minus* f. 6v. At Stuttgart. Annus holding the Sun and the Moon in his hands (p. 24)

b. *(above right)* The Cathedral of St. Lazarus, Autun. Arch above west doorway of the nave. Medallions 16-22—See pp. 30-31 of the above book

c. *(left)* Scorpio (24) and October (25)

d. *(below)* Cancer (16) and June (17)

16. a. West end of the face of the south doorway.

b. Underside

Confronted Figures

17. a. St. Andrew's Church, Bredwardine, Herefordshire. North doorway

b. Lavardin nr. Montoire (Loir et Cher). Capitals of pillars of the choir arcade. South side, south face

c. The same, north side, south face

18. a. Illustration No. 6 in Mr. G. Marshall's book on Hereford Cathedral

b. Photograph taken with the aid of flash in May 1963

c. Photograph taken after the removal. The tympanum is now in the north-east transept

Tree Motif

19. a. St. Michael's Church, High Ercall, Salop.
Tympanum reset in north wall of nave

b. *(left)* St. Mary's Church, Dymock,
Gloucestershire. South doorway of the
nave
c. (*below*) St. Mary's Church, Kempley,
Gloucestershire. South doorway of the
nave

20. a. St. Peter's Church,
Newnham-on-Severn, Gloucestershire. Loose
damaged tympanum now situated near the
pupit in the nave

b. St. Peter's Church, Bromyard, Herefordshire. Font
situated at the west end of the nave

c. St. Michael's Church,
Rochford, Worcestershire-
lately Herefordshire. North
doorway of the nave, now
blocked

21. a. Disused Chapel, Yatton, Herefordshire (ruined condition). South doorway of the nave

b. St. Mary and St. David's Church, Kilpeck, Herefordshire. South doorway of the nave

c. The Ruined Abbey, Buildwas, Salop. Keyser, (b) p. xxxvii, says that it is in the little cloister adjoining the Abbot's House

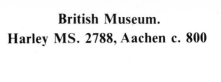

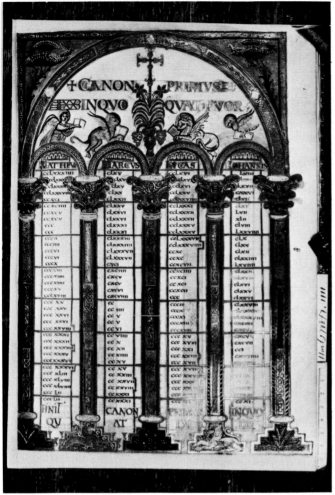

22. a. f.7r

b. f.6v

Tympana with the Agnus Dei Motif

23. a. St. John Baptist Church, Preston nr. Dymock, Gloucestershire. North doorway of the nave

b. St. Mary's Church, Byton, Herefordshire. Reset tympanum, south wall of the organ chamber

c. St. Gregory's Church, Castle Moreton, Worcestershire. North doorway of the nave

24. a. St. Mary's Church, Upleadon,
Gloucestershire. North doorway of the nave.

b. St. Giles Church, Aston, Worcestershire.
North doorway of the nave

c. St. Nicholas Church, Gloucester. South
doorway of the nave

Rams' Heads at Corners of Capital

25. a. National Museum, Ravenna

b. St. Mark's Venice. Nave capital

c. and d. La Trinité, Caen. Capitals at nave crossing. Photographs of plates in J. S. Cotman's Architectural Antiquities of Normandy (1822). Plate 28

Rams-Head Capital in Hereford Cathedral

26. a. and b. This loose capital is now in the Vicars' cloister

Capitals with Step Pattern and Volute

27. a. The so-called Palace of Theodoric, Ravenna. In foliage form; entrance today.

b. Worms Cathedral. In foliage form. Plinth of pier

c. St. John Baptist's Church, Preston nr. Dymock, Gloucestershire. Loose capital of pillar piscina. Now in Gloucester Museum

28. a. St. Mary's Church, Dymock, Gloucestershire. South doorway of the nave, west side

b. St. John's Church, Pauntley, Gloucestershire. South doorway of the nave, west side

29. a. St. Bridget's Church, Bridstow,
Herefordshire. South side of the chancel arch

b. St. Mary's Church, Kempley, Gloucestershire.
North side of the chancel arch

c. St. John's Church, Pauntley, Gloucestershire.
South side of the chancel arch

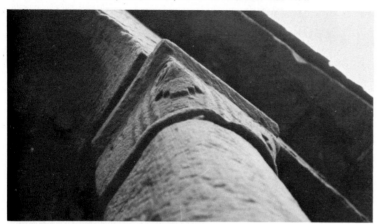

30. a. St. Mary's Church, Fownhope, Herefordshire. Third stage of the central tower, south face, external and internal view

b. North face, internal view

c. St. Peter's Church, Newnham-on-Severn, Gloucestershire. Loose capital on the sill of a north window in the nave

31. a. St. Michael's Church, Bulley, Gloucestershire.
South doorway of the nave, west side

b. East side

c. St. Andrew's Church, Churcham, Gloucestershire.
South wall of the nave

Small Confronted Volutes

32. a. St. Mary's Church, Dymock, Gloucestershire. Capital at the north-east corner of the old central tower block. The tower has been destroyed

b. St. Mary's Church, Kempley,
Gloucestershire. Capital at the south
doorway of the nave, east side

c. St. Peter's Church, Newnham-on-Severn,
Gloucestershire. Loose capital now on the sill of
a south window in the nave

33. a. St. Peter's Church, Rowlstone, Herefordshire. Chancel arch, north side

b. The Priory of St. Peter and St. Paul, Leominster, Herefordshire. West doorway of the nave, inside

c. The same capital, north side

String Course

34. a. Hereford Cathedral. South wall of vestry, internal

b. South wall of chancel aisle, south side

c. St. Mary's Church, Monmouth. West wall of north-west tower

d. St. John Baptist Church, Letton, Herefordshire. North wall of the nave

b. Continuation of a.

35. a. St. Mary's Church, Linton, Herefordshire.
This short length of string course is at the west
end of the north wall of the nave, now forming
the south wall of the later north aisle.

c. St. Mary's Church, Dymock, Gloucestershire. All are on
the south side. Base of blind arcading of chancel

d. Nave towards the west end

e. Destroyed old tower block

36. a. St. Mary's Church, Dymock,
Gloucestershire. North wall of the nave

b. North wall of the chancel interior

The Step Pattern

37. a. St. Mary's Priory Church, Deerhurst, Gloucestershire
Madonna and Child over tower middle arch (child would
have been painful in the oval supported by the Madonna's
hands).

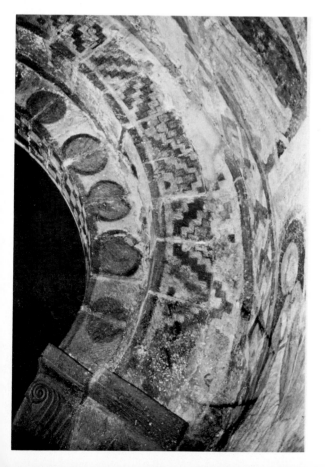

b. St. Mary's Church, Kempley, Gloucestershire.
Paintings (12c) on the east face of the chancel arch

The Step Pattern divorced from the Volute

38. a. St. John Baptist Church, Eldersfield, Worcestershire. Chancel arch, north side

b. South doorway of the nave, west side. A later doorway had been built within the original 12th-century entrance

c. St. John Baptist Church, Beckford, Worcestershire. South doorway of the nave, east side

39. a. The Church of St. James the Great, Stoke Orchard, Gloucestershire.
Font

b. Hereford Cathedral. Nave Capital,
south side

c. St. Mary's Church, Upleadon,
Gloucestershire. North doorway of the nave,
east side

Knot Motif

40. a. 'Sculptural Crosses' Athens. This is a photograph of plate 219 of vol. 2 of N.H.J. Westlake's *The History of Design in Mural Painting from the Earliest Time to the 12th century*

b. St. Mark's Cathedral, Venice. This motif is carved upon several capitals in the crypt under the sanctuary

c. St. Deinst Church, Llangarron, Herefordshire. Reused stone in the south-east buttress of the sanctuary. See also the two examples on the Byton (Herefordshire) reused tympanum, Plate 23b

Knot Motif?

41. a. St. Peter's Church, Rowlstone, Herefordshire. South doorway of the nave, east side

42. a. The ruined Chapel of Yatton, Herefordshire. South doorway of the nave, west side

b. South doorway of the nave, east side

c. St. Bridget's Church, Bridstow, Herefordshire. North side of the chancel arch

Arcaded Fonts

43. a. Hereford Cathedral. This font was damaged at the time of the fall of the west front in 1786

b. Mitcheldean, Gloucestershire. The top half was destroyed at an unknown date, and later renewed. The join is obvious. The new portion, it is said, was modelled on the Newnham-on-Severn font

c. Newnham-on-Severn, Gloucestershire. This font, too, suffered damage in the 19th-century fire, see page 38. A similar font may also be seen in Rendcombe Church, Gloucestershire

Carved Stones at heads of Windows—
Tympana Type

44. a. St. Andrew's Church, Tangmere, Sussex. Courtesy of the Courtauld Institute of Art

b. St. Mary's Church, Stoke-sub-Hamdon, Somerset Courtesy of the Courtauld Institute of Art

c. St. Philip and St. James Church, Tarrington, Herefordshire. North wall of the chancel

Windows

45. a. Bishop's Chapel, Hereford (late 11th century). External splay of north-east window, now within the south alley of the Bishop's Cloister

b. St. Mary's Church, Kempley, Gloucestershire. Outside splay of north window in the chancel

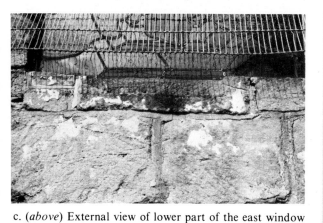

c. (*above*) External view of lower part of the east window of the chancel. Note the sill of earlier east window in the centre—cf sill of window on b.

d. (*right*) St. Andrew's Church, Churcham, Gloucestershire. South window (outside splay) of the west tower, lowest stage

46. a. (left) St. Peter's Church, Newnham-on-Severn, Gloucestershire. Reused over the present north doorway of the nave

b. (below) St. Peter's Church, Peterchurch, Herefordshire. North wall of the nave. The three narrow lights have much tufa material in their facings

c. (left) St. James Church, Tedstone-Delamere, Herefordshire. South-west window in the nave

d. (above) St. Mary's Church, Kempley, Gloucestershire-Windows at east end. See text

Miscellaneous Monuments

47. a. St. Mary's Church, Upleadon, Gloucestershire. Mask above the chancel arch, east face

b. St. Peter's Church, Newnham-on-Severn, Gloucestershire. Loose (damaged) capital on window sill in nave ·

c. St. John Baptist Church, Preston nr. Dymock, Gloucestershire. twin headed corbel at north-west corner of the nave

Entrances to Turret Stairways

48. a. and b. St. Mary's Church, Dymock, Gloucestershire. In the north wall of the old (destroyed) central tower block. a. internal; b. external

c. St. Michael and All Angels Church, Ledbury, Herefordshire. In west wall of the nave This doorway leads into a stairway encased, externally, by the later face of the west wall

d. St. John the Evangelist Church, Milborne Port, Somerset. In the angle between the south transept and the nave

Apsidal Churches

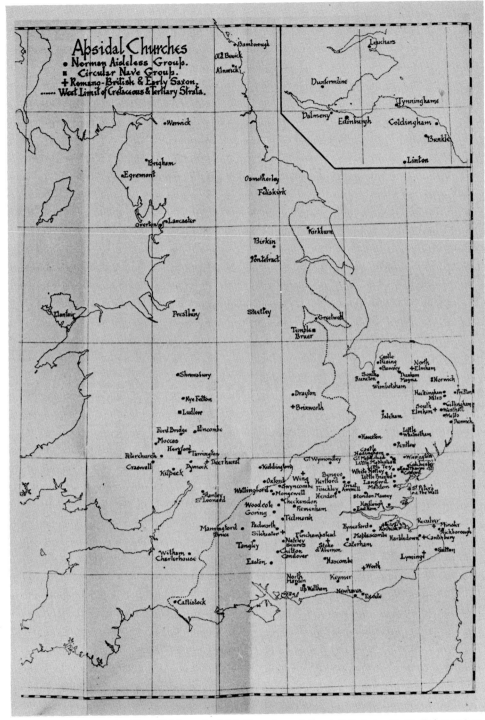

49. Location map in *The Aisleless Apsidal Churches of Great Britain* by F. H. Fairweather

Dymock—St. Mary's. Evidence of Apsidel East End

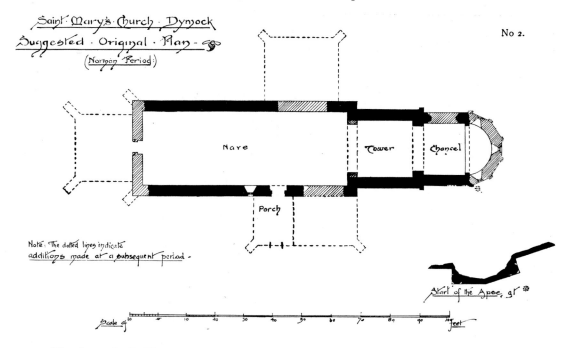

Saint Mary's Church Dymock
Suggested · Original · Plan -
(Norman Period:)

No 2.

Nave

Tower

Chancel

Porch

Note: The dotted lines indicate additions made at a subsequent period -

Start of the Apse, gr *

Scale of feet

Plan drawn by F. W. Waller, Esq. Reproduced by courtesy of Colonel N. H. Waller, M.C., T.D. and the Cotteswold Naturalists' Field Club

50. a. Page 45 of *Dymock Down the Ages,* (Gloucester 1966) by J. E. Gethyn-Jones

b. South wall of chancel

c. North wall. Now inside the Priest's vestry

Apses

51. a. St. Michael and All Angels Church,
Moccas, Herefordshire

b. St. Peter's Church, Peterchurch,
Herefordshire

c. St. Mary and St. David's Church, Kilpeck, Herefordshire

52. a. North doorway of the nave

b. South doorway of the nave, west side

c. East side

53. a. Cross fixed to south wall of the tower, on the inside of the lowest stage (vestry). This may have been the ridge cross at the west end of the nave

b. Consecration Cross? East face of the chancel arch, south side

c. Original west doorway. This, now, is within the lowest stage (vestry) of the 13th-century tower

54. Chancel Arch

St. Mary's Church, Dymock, Gloucestershire

55. a. North wall of the nave. Pilasters and String Course. The string course on this side, apart from a shamfered lower half, is plain

b. South respond of the broken arch between the chancel arch and the destroyed apse. The bases of these nook shafts are enriched with scale pattern

c. North respond. The bases of these nook shafts are enriched with spur motif

Doorways—Complete

56. a. St. John's Church, Pauntley, Gloucestershire.
South nave

b. St. Michael's Church, Castle Frome, Herefordshire.
South chancel

c. The ruined Chapel of Yatton, Herefordshire.
South nave

57. a. (*left*) St. Mary's Priory Church, Deerhurst, Gloucestershire
b. (*below*) St. Anne's Church, Oxenhall, Gloucestershire

c. St. John Baptist Church, Whitbourne, Herefordshire

South Doorway of St. Mary's Church, Dymock, Gloucestershire

58. a. (*above left*) General view. See also 19b.
b. (*above right*) West side
c. (*left*) West side
d. East side

St. Michael's Church, Moccas, Herefordshire

59. a. (*above*) North doorway
b. (*right*) South doorway
c. South doorway, west side

60. a. (*above*) and b. (*right*) St. Michael's Church, Moccas, Herefordshire. These are photographs of earlier photographs showing their condition more than 50 years ago. a. South doorway and tympanum; b. North doorway and tympanum

c. Moccas chancel arch

d. St. Peter's Church, Peterchurch, Herefordshire. Chancel arch, south side

61. a. St. Peter's Church, Bromyard, Herefordshire. Reverse of Plate 20b

b. St. Michael and All Angels Church, Ledbury, Herefordshire. See text p27.

Note: Anglo-Norman pillar base overlaid by the Early English.

62. a. (*above left*) Chepstow Castle, Monmouthshire. West
wall of keep
b. (*above right*) St. Mary's Church, Linton, Herefordshire.
Pillar of north arcade in the nave
c. (*left*) St. Andrew's Church, Coln Rogers, Gloucestershire.
Pilaster on north wall